Do Not Remove
Private Property.

Bet ☐ **W9-BUL-401**

c/o Rita HAMILTON
Room # 1
Param House ?R

713 - 78 HILLY ST.,
Toronto ONT.,
M4S - 3C9

If This Book decides to Roam Please
Box its ears or send it home
Thank you

Rita Hamilton.

ARTISTS ABOVE ALL

Marc Alexander

Men and women who triumphed over adversity through their art

Erich Stegmann Burano, Venetian Lagoon

Mouth and Foot Painting Artists, North America

Text © 2005 Marc Alexander

Paintings © Association of Mouth and Foot Painting Artists

Printed in Germany

ISBN 0-9771148-0-5

"Your work inspires us to embrace our dreams, to dispense with the ordinary and creates a vision for us all to share."

Al Gore, Former U.S. Vice President

This book is dedicated to the artists who made it possible.

The Artists

PAST MASTERS

Myron Angus   p23

Christy Brown   p26

Charles Fowler   p28

Bruce Peardon   p31

Erich Stegmann   p33

Marlyse Tovae   p36

NORTH AMERICAN ARTISTS

Cindi Bernhardt   p61

Edward Brill   p63

Dennis Francesconi   p65

Stephen Fuller   p69

Michel Guillemette   p71

Lynda Hamilton   p73

Ann Harrison-May   p75

Isabelle Jackson   p77

Jeffrey LaDow   p79

Daniel Laflamme   p109

Nancy Rae Litteral   p111

Susie Matthias   p113

Jean Michalski   p115

David Nolt   p117

Stanley Obritski   p119

Janice "Penny" Oman   p121

Jack Reich   p123

Jimmy Rodolfos   p125

Steven Sles   p128

Robert E. Smith   p131

Robert Thome   p133

Cody Tresierra   p135

Brom Wikstrom   p137

OVERSEAS ARTISTS

Iwao Adachi   p143

Glenn Barnett   p146

Eros Bonamini   p149

Ruth Christensen   p151

Kun-Shan Hsieh   p153

Soon-Yi Oh   p155

Jayantilal Shihora   p157

Cristobal Toledo   p159

José Uribe   p181

Trevor Wells   p184

THE ARTISTS

7

Introduction

This book is made up of success stories. They tell of the triumph of the human spirit over odds that at times must have seemed impossible to these men and women who, despite the fact they are without the use of their hands, succeeded in achieving independence through artistic endeavor.

Although victims of illness or accident, they are the most positive people one could wish to meet and there is nothing depressing to be found in these pages, on the contrary.

All are members of the Association of Mouth and Foot Painting Artists which enables them to follow their careers by marketing their creative work as greeting cards, calendars, prints and similar artistic products.

The Association is one of the world's most remarkable self-help organizations. It is the dream-come-true of a visionary German artist named Erich Stegmann whose story is told further on. He was born in Darmstadt in 1912 and when two years old he was stricken by Infantile Paralysis, as poliomyelitis was then called. He survived the initial attack but was left without the use of his arms and hands while his legs were affected so that he could only walk short distances. When he started school he was determined to keep up with his able-bodied classmates and to this end he taught himself to write and draw by holding a pencil in his mouth. Painting became the most important thing in his young life and after attending art college he became a professional artist. His work appeared in exhibitions and he had the satisfaction of knowing that his pictures sold because of their quality and not because of the unusual way they were produced.

His career suffered badly due to his opposition to the Nazi regime and this resulted in a period in prison but after the war he re-established himself as an artist and also as a successful publisher. It was then that he was able to concentrate on a long-cherished project. He once declared, 'There are people all over the world handicapped like me who have the ability to paint yet have to depend on their families or social security payments to survive.

'The trouble is that while they may be talented, most of them would need to have proper tuition to get them up to a professional standard and that is something which few can afford. If only they could organize. With proper marketing their best work could be sold as cards and prints. Everyone would get an equal share of the proceeds and there would be scholarships for those who need to have their talents developed.

'I want to form an organization – an international partnership – of artists who paint either with their mouths or feet. There will have to be several basic rules. For one thing everyone who becomes a member must have a standard of work that an independent panel considers equal to that of non-handicapped professional painters. It will be a co-operative governed entirely by its members and will be a proper commercial enterprise. It must never, never be thought of as a charity. If people buy its prints and cards because they feel sorry for handicapped artists the project fails. Its products must be sold on merit alone.'

Erich's partnership was set up in 1956 and in March of the following year its sixteen founding members met for the first time at Liechtenstein's Wald Hotel. When Erich departed this life in 1984 the membership had risen to around two hundred painters in 37 countries. Today it is more than six hundred in over 60 countries.

Apart from working tirelessly to get the new organization established, Erich constantly

Erich Stegmann
Mona Lisa (Copy from original by
Leonardo da Vinci)

Erich Stegmann   Fishermen's Cottages, Madagascar

INTRODUCTION

Erich Stegmann Bicycle Man

sought new members, and today the Association carries on that tradition. When contact is made with a disabled person who appears to have artistic potential, his or her work is evaluated and if it is considered sufficiently promising a scholarship is offered. Students receive stipends to assist them in furthering their talents with painting materials, tuition and specially designed equipment if necessary. This may include electric wheelchairs or vans adapted to carry them which are often beyond the means of the handicapped surviving on state benefits.

Anyone who has lost the use of their hands and paints by holding the brush in their mouth or with their feet, irrespective of race, creed or color, is eligible for consideration by the MFPA. There are three qualifying levels – Student Member, Associate Member and Full Member. To maintain constantly high standards, artists must attain a level of expertise that will satisfy the critical examination of a panel of art specialists before they are promoted to a higher level. Full membership is granted when a mouth or foot painter's work is judged to be equal to that of able-bodied professional artists.

The MFPA partnerships in the United States and Canada are members of the international Association based in Liechtenstein. Erich Stegmann chose the Principality because of its political neutrality and the advantages of the internationally acceptable Swiss Franc. The Association is a 'democratic co-operative', all its artists having a voice in how it is run by electing delegates to represent their interests.

According to the Association's statutes a Delegates' Convention must be held every three years though in practice it takes place more frequently. This Convention is responsible for control of all the Association's activities and appoints the Managing Board which oversees the work of the few able-bodied administration and professional staff employed by the organization.

Erich Stegmann was deeply aware of the disabled artist's fear that deteriorating health would put an end to his or her painting career and the income derived from it. To eliminate this anxiety it was decreed that when an artist progressed from being a student to full membership the monthly income this provided was for life regardless of whether increasing disability prevented the member from producing pictures that the Association could market. As one member recently remarked, 'What other organization would continue to keep you on the payroll when you could no longer work!'

Most of the time disabled painters work alone and understandably they can be liable to feelings of isolation. To counter this Erich Stegmann inaugurated international conventions as an important aspect of the Association's activities. At such get-togethers the work of the Association is discussed, there are workshops where experts give helpful advice to the artists as they paint, visits are arranged to famous art galleries and social functions organized for the mostly wheelchair-bound guests. Old friendships are renewed, there is much animated conversation and an equal amount of laughter.

These meetings are held in different major cities of the world as another of Erich Stegmann's enthusiasms was travel. In his day it was difficult for those confined to wheelchairs to make long journeys, but by arranging these meetings in different countries he set out to encourage more enlightened attitudes towards handicapped travelers. Indeed, he has been described as the pioneer of travel for the disabled.

An example of one such meeting as Erich Stegmann had envisaged took place in 2003 when the MFPA held its biggest ever international art exhibition in the U.S.A. at the Woodruff Arts Center, Atlanta, where more than 130 paintings from mouth and foot artists from many countries were exhibited. Over fifty American and twelve Canadian artists attended the week-long event with their carers and family members. In painting workshops they were given professional advice on their techniques by visiting able-bodied artists, and they took part in a conference to which MFPA Board members traveled from all over the world.

The exhibition was opened by Mr. Al Gore, former U.S. Vice President, who said of the

Association, 'This is not a charity. These artists earn their own way. They pay their own way in life and help their fellow artists while they are at it. They make a good living, thank you very much, and they are proud to be taxpayers and they are proud to be helping others.'

As I walked around the exhibition the adage 'Every picture tells a story' came to my mind. What stories of pain and courage, enthusiasm and achievement lay behind these canvases!

And laughter! Good humor is something these artists have in common and though I have met many mouth and foot painters, I cannot recall one who bemoaned his or her fate. They share this quality as they share their love of art. In other respects their backgrounds, ages, philosophies and beliefs are all different as the stories in this book will prove.

Marc Alexander

Erich Stegmann   Self Portrait

Myron Angus
Summer by the Lake

Myron Angus
Woodland Mist

Overleaf:
Charles Fowler
Trees in Blossom,
Southern France

Charles Fowler   Herm & Jethou, from Sark, Channel Islands

Charles Fowler   Small Lake

Bruce Peardon
The Sleepy Fisher

Bruce Peardon By the Coast

Christy Brown
Snowed-in Village

Marlyse Tovae   Colorful Display

Marlyse Tovae Ships at Harbor

Past Masters

Some of the mouth and foot painting artists who contributed so much to their partnership and whose inspiration lives on in their paintings.

Myron Angus

"My work became my passion."

It was a day in 1933 and a line of eager people were lined up in a Toronto exhibition hall, each clutching a book entitled "My Desire". A signing session had been arranged for the remarkable author Bill Watson. One after another the purchasers of his book laid it open on the table at which he was sitting and with a smile he signed – with a pen held in his mouth. It was the same method by which the armless author had written the book which made such a stir.

Among those who watched fascinated was a couple who had a passionate interest in what they saw, and when the first rush of book buyers had departed with their uniquely signed copies, they approached the author. Introducing themselves as Mr. and Mrs. Angus from St. Mary's, they explained that when their son Myron had been born seven years earlier his hands, arms and legs were completely paralyzed. All he could do was sit at home, frustrated at not being able to play like the other children he saw from his window or go to school.

Could Mr. Watson, from his own experience of disability, proffer any advice? Bill Watson certainly could.

First of all he autographed a copy of his book specially for Myron and then he said, 'Put a pencil between his teeth. Let him hold it on either the left or right side, whichever way is the most comfortable, and let him learn to write with it. And once he has mastered that, put him in school – they can't refuse to teach him.'

On their journey back to St. Mary's the couple eagerly discussed what they had seen and been told. At last it seemed there was a glimmer of hope for Myron. If a man who had no arms had managed to write a book it might be possible for their son to receive a normal education.

Back at home Myron was given the book "My Desire" as proof of what might be accomplished and his father bought pencils and pads by the dozen for the boy to attempt to form letters. As with so many mouth painters, the first attempts at controlling a pencil or brush clamped between the teeth was often disappointing. For one thing the eyes have to be so close to the paper that it is difficult to get an overall picture of what one is doing and eye strain is a common complaint with those who are forced to write and draw by this method.

Then there is the question of control. Just when it seems that a word has been written satisfactorily an involuntary head movement will send the pencil point skidding off at a tangent. But even at the age of seven Myron was aware of how necessary his 'feeble attempts' – as he later called them – were if he was going to free himself from the limitations of disability. He never gave up trying and was rewarded by the ability to write as clearly as his non-handicapped peers.

'It was as if a new door had suddenly opened in front of me,' Myron told the author. 'And I was lucky to go to a regular school. I think it is a big thing not to get labeled as "different".'

His success as a student at High School, where everyone else was able-bodied, was recognized in 1940 when he was awarded a medal inscribed with the words 'For Moral Courage'.

Later the Angus family moved to Toronto where Myron was to complete his formal education at Riverdale Collegiate. In those days the needs of the disabled were not as widely recognized as today and the college did not have the facilities for students such as Myron. However, the staff went out of their way to accommodate him and he was actually carried from room to room.

During this period Myron had become increasingly interested in the idea of drawing and painting. He dearly wanted to attend an art school so that his attempts with a mouth-held brush could be given professional guidance but, as with his college, art establishments were not geared to the requirements of someone so disabled and were not as sympathetic as the Riverdale Collegiate.

'I was fascinated with color, line and form,' he later recalled. 'And as I was unable to receive formal art training I set about teaching myself, at first by copying illustrations in the family Bible and the works of Old Masters. I was determined to settle for no less than my best and my work became my passion.'

When he finished college he was single-minded in his efforts to obtain employment in order to support himself, not necessarily the easiest objective for someone wheelchair-bound without the use of their arms.

Yet he managed, and in this it was his enthusiasm for painting that clinched the job. He started work in a garage looking after the books with a mouth-held pen – and painting lettering and logos on the door panels of trucks.

Many a truck owner was astonished to walk into the busy garage to see a young man in a wheelchair with a long-handled brush in his mouth decorating the side of his vehicle. It might not have been art as taught in colleges but it certainly gave Myron a sense of self confidence. Yet while he added up figures and did sign-painting during his working hours he continued to practice at what he believed was his true vocation – to become a professional artist.

In 1948 he felt he had progressed enough to mount his first exhibition. It was held in a gallery in Yonge Street, Toronto, and was an instant success. So many people wanted to see the work of the young mouth painter that lines formed in the street. Stories appeared in the Press not only about the technique he used but praising his delicate landscapes that reflected his love of the lakes and woods around Toronto.

Other exhibitions followed in major cities in Canada and the USA.

Eleven years after his first exhibition Myron bought the gallery on Yonge Street where he not only exhibited and sold his own works but also those of artists who had suffered disability like himself. The gallery proved to be a success, and it needed to be because Myron had married and he and his wife Alma had a young family to care for.

In 1963 news of Myron and his work crossed the Atlantic and came to the attention of the Association of Mouth and Foot Painting Artists at its headquarters in Liechtenstein. Samples of his work were requested and the independent committee of experts who appraise the work of potential members was duly impressed. The next year Myron was elected a full member of the Association.

One result of this was that he found himself helping to organize an MFPA exhibition at Toronto's Casa Loma during October 1965. At this exhibition 150 paintings by the Association's members were put on display. It gave Myron the opportunity to meet the organization's founder Erich Stegmann who, as a living example of how the disabled can rise above their physical adversities, received an ovation from the guests at the preview.

Four years later Myron found himself flying to India as the representative of Canadian and United States mouth and foot painting artists for a Delegates' Convention being held in Bombay. The artist had come a long way since the days he painted signs on trucks.

Thanks to the financial independence gained as a result of MFPA membership Myron was able to give up the running of his gallery and devote his whole attention to art and a venture that had long occupied his thoughts. Mindful of his own early struggles to overcome the handicap that fate had laid upon him, he wished to help handicapped people to lead fuller lives. To do this he planned to travel about Canada giving lectures and demonstrations that would encourage the disabled and at the same time give the able-bodied a better understanding of those less physically fortunate than themselves.

Rehabilitation centers, children's hospitals, service clubs, church groups, schools and jails all provided venues for Myron's message, the only problem was that traveling by train and plane was expensive and difficult, especially as at that time most hotels were not accessible for wheelchairs. Then a friend suggested that a motorhome might be the answer, and it proved to be the ideal means of travel for his unique roadshow. For over twenty years – helped by Alma, his daughter Theresa and sons Earl and Kevin – he devoted his spare time to his crusade in the cause of the disabled.

Myron also served on the Ontario Advisory Council for the Physically Disabled. As a result of these activities he received many awards including the Vanier Medal for his achievements

in painting, penmanship, and humanitarian services, and the Legion des Gens Coeur from Paris for human courage.

At his home in Port Stanley, Ontario, Myron continued to paint with undiminished enthusiasm, though as he grew older he used water colors because they are lighter to apply than oils which put a strain on his teeth while gripping the brush. He often worked under the critical gaze of his beautiful Siamese cat who, while accepting that Myron was unable to stroke him, compromised by raising his chin so that his neck could be tickled with the end of a mouth stick.

Myron Angus, the doyen of the Canadian mouth and foot painting artists, died in 2003, leaving a legacy of memorable works of art and younger artists he had inspired to become the 'able disabled'.

Myron Angus meeting the late Pope John Paul II

Christy Brown

"Painting became everything to me."

Christy Brown found fame as the author of 'My Left Foot' that was later made into a film of the same name and which won world-wide acclaim. What is not generally known is that he became a member of the Association of Mouth and Foot Painting Artists, receiving encouragement and financial support until his unexpected death in 1981.

Born in Dublin, Ireland in 1932, Christy suffered from cerebral palsy which caused paralysis in his arms and legs. In his biography he described growing up in a large poverty-stricken family unable to do anything for himself.

It was a frustrating life for the boy, unable to play games with his brothers or later on go to school to learn to read and write like the normal children in the street. Then, in a moving passage in his biography, he described how he managed to use his toes to grip a piece of yellow chalk which his sisters had been using to do their sums. After a struggle he managed to print the letter A on the floor.

'That one letter... was my road to a new world, my key to mental freedom,' he wrote later. 'It was to provide a source of relaxation to the tense, taut thing that was me which panted for expression behind a twisted mouth.'

After this initial success Christy worked desperately to write with his foot, getting his brothers and sisters to show him how words were spelled and which he endeavored to copy. Finally he did manage to print his first word, and it made a highly dramatic moment in the film when he wrote MOTHER.

As he grew older, when he had mastered the technique of using his left foot as a hand, Christy turned to drawing and painting to fill in the lonely hours while his brothers and sisters were at school. When he was twelve the Sunday Independent ran a Christmas painting competition in the form of a black and white scene from the Cinderella story which had to be colored in by young readers. Christy painstakingly applied the color – and won.

This success, minor though it might have seemed to an able-bodied child, was a tremendous encouragement and from then on painting became a vital part of his life as these words he later wrote testify: 'Painting became everything to me. By it I learned to express myself in many subtle ways. Through it I made articulate all that I saw and felt, all that went on inside the mind that was housed within my useless body like a prisoner in a cell looking out on a world that hadn't become a reality to me.'

One day when Christy was in his early twenties there was a knock at the door of his parents' house. When his mother opened the door she saw two strangers. One was short with remarkably blue eyes and hands that were to remain tucked neatly into the pockets of his suit for the whole of the visit. His companion said, 'This is Herr Erich Stegmann. As he does not speak English I have come as his interpreter. He has come a long way to see Mr. Christy Brown.'

A puzzled Mrs. Brown led the mysterious visitors to the shed at the back of the house where Christy sat in his wheelchair and passed his days with his brush and paints.

Once the strangers were seated inside the shed Christy listened in near disbelief while the interpreter explained, 'Herr Stegmann wishes to meet artists, who like you, are unable to paint with their hands but hold their brushes with their mouths or with their toes. He is a mouth painter himself and he has come from Munich especially to meet you.'

Then Erich Stegmann said through the interpreter, 'This year I have founded an international co-operative of disabled artists who, because they are isolated by their physical condition, are unable to get a fair financial return for their work. I have long believed that if such artists could be organized into a co-operative, proceeds from having their work published could be shared equally amongst them. Of course such work would have to be of a high standard but who has artistic potential we offer him or her a scholarship so that they can afford proper art materials and receive tuition.

'The project has been launched in Liechtenstein with sixteen members but I am seeking more people with artistic talent to join us. When word reached me that there is a mouth painter in Dublin I came to find you. Handicapped painters who join our Association provide paintings that are suitable for greetings cards and calendars, and in return they receive a regular income for life regardless of whether increasing disability makes it impossible for them to continue producing work for us to publish. That is one of our most important rules. Our members must be able to concentrate on their art without feeling uneasy about the future.

'Now I should be very interested in seeing your work,' Erich Stegmann concluded.

Christy could hardly believe what the interpreter was saying. This visit was so unexpected and could mean a turning point in his life.

It became obvious that the visitor could not use his hands – the result of poliomyelitis as a baby – as the interpreter had to hold up examples of Christy's painting for him to see. He regarded the work with a highly critical gaze and while Christy sat tense, wondering what his verdict would be. If he was accepted into this partnership it would not only mean a regular income but the chance of having his pictures seen by people outside his family circle – the chance to become a recognized artist.

At length the last picture was put aside and Erich Stegmann turned to Christy and said, 'Welcome to the Association.'

From then on Christy enjoyed an independence that he had not known before and encouragement in his work that caused him to write later in My Left Foot: 'Painting became the great love in my life, the main pivot of my concentration. I lived within the orbit of my paints and brushes.' In many ways he was speaking for the hundreds of disabled artists who have struggled to express themselves by means of paint brushes gripped in their teeth or held in their toes.

Charles Fowler

"The quality of acceptance."

In Britain many members of the Mouth and Foot Painting Artists' Association remember Charles Fowler with special affection. Not only was this tall, elegant man an accomplished artist but he was a special friend to those aspiring to join the Association and those who had been accepted as students. It was not unusual for a student's telephone to ring and Charles would be on the line to ask how he or she was progressing, give words of encouragement and, if necessary, practical advice.

A lesser known aspect of Charles' character was that he believed he had a psychic streak.

'There is no doubt that I did dream my accident although it was a day out,' he once told the author. 'When I was eighteen I had a dream in which I saw myself covered with blood on a railway track. And above the scene I saw the words Beware of Wednesday. Needless to say I was very careful on the following Wednesday when I alighted from the train on which I commuted from Wimbledon to London where I was a clerk. But the next day, being in a hurry to meet a friend, I opened the door of the carriage too quickly with the result I slipped and fell between the platform and the railway line. The wheels of the train amputated my arms above the elbows.

'I had to stay in hospital for two months but I found it less difficult than you might imagine. It was a great nuisance of course, but I was very young and therefore it was easier for me to adapt than if I had been twenty-five or thirty. And I was helped by the sheer sense of not worrying. I had the quality of acceptance, as indeed most disabled people have.'

Charles's easy-going attitude to life went back to his happy home life in the Chelsea suburb of London where he had been born. An only child,

his natural cheerfulness protected him against the prejudice that was sometimes levelled at such children. He enjoyed school where his favorite subject was art and for which he received several prizes that made him consider the possibility of attending an art school. This did not eventuate; instead he became a clerk with a linseed oil firm in Mincing Lane, which is in the heart of London's financial district known as the City. Each day he commuted to work by train from Wimbledon where his parents now lived.

While the young man thus accepted the fact that he had lost both his arms it did not mean he was going to resign himself to inactivity mental or otherwise.

'I think one of the best things I ever did was to say to myself, "When I can leave hospital I'm not going to go home in a car, I'm going to walk back,"' he said. True to his promise to himself he did walk home when he was discharged.

At school Charles' favorite subject was art and when he was back with his parents his old interest in painting reasserted itself. It seemed the only thing to do was to hold his brush between his teeth.

'There was no other way of doing it,' he explained. 'As I said I was very adaptable then. And compared with so many mouth and foot artists, I am extremely lucky in that I do not have a breathing problem and I can walk.'

A picture of a tulip in a vase was the subject of his first attempt, and it was not long afterwards that he painted a May tree in blossom. There was something about this picture that caught the imaginations of those who saw it, so much so that a number of friends and acquaintances all asked to buy it. This interest in his work inspired Charles to set up a May tree production line in which he worked on seven paintings simultaneously. There is nothing more encouraging for a novice artist than to receive cash for his or her paintings and it was this that decided Charles to take up art as a career.

He began by taking basic lessons from a professional artist which meant making a rail journey from Wimbledon Station. Despite the fact it had been the scene of his accident Charles made up his mind to travel alone and to this end he developed a technique for opening the doors of railway carriages with his foot.

Later it was arranged for Charles to be enrolled in an art school. He wondered how he would be received on his first day but it turned out to be better than he expected. When he was sent to the life room everyone turned to look at him when he walked in. No one spoke but the question in all minds was what was a man without arms doing in their classroom. Unperturbed, Charles picked up a pencil in his teeth and calmly started sketching with skill and confidence.

'After that I was ignored as an oddity and accepted as a student who could draw,' Charles said.

After four years at art school Charles won the Ministry of Education's Award of High Merit after which he won an Exhibition Scholarship to the Royal College of Art where, after another four years, he gained his diploma. Although his work had already been exhibited in galleries ranging from the Royal Academy to the Royal Society of Painting in Water Color, his priority was to find work that would give him a regular income. He managed to obtain a post in the Farnham School of Art teaching Still Life.

On the first day at the school the principal introduced Charles to the class.

'Do not be nervous of Mr. Fowler,' he said and, as smoking was not then the Eighth Deadly Sin, added that it would be a kindness if someone would light a cigarette for him if he needed it. Halfway through his lecture Charles did feel he needed a smoke and a student dutifully took a cigarette from the packet in Charles's pocket, lit

it and placed it between Charles's lips. Feeling more relaxed Charles continued to expound on Still Life until the cigarette had burned uncomfortably close to his mouth so that with a toss of his head he flicked it neatly into a wastepaper container.

Woosh!

The container, which was full of turpentine-soaked rags, erupted into a pillar of fire.

'It was a spectacular way of beginning a teaching career,' Charles told the story with a smile that suggested he enjoyed such an introduction to his class as it put a little drama into Still Life.

During holiday periods Charles traveled extensively to unspoilt spots which he captured on his canvases.

'I am an Atlantic rather than a Mediterranean person,' he once explained. 'I like to feel the power of the wind and watch the movement of the sea. If there is nobody around I will paint on the spot. After all this time, I still get a little unsure when I know there are people watching me. I know it's silly but I'm not like Erich Stegmann who couldn't have cared less who was watching him.'

In 1975 Charles retired from formal teaching and planned to concentrate on his own art work.

'You should get in touch with the Association of Mouth and Foot Painting Artists,' a friend suggested.

'Never heard of it,' Charles replied but the thought of such an organization intrigued him. He went to the Association's office in London to learn more and as a result submitted eight water-colors. The evaluating panel was so impressed by the quality of these paintings that Charles was granted full membership immediately.

From then on his work was not only used for Christmas cards that were popular around the world but he dedicated himself to helping fellow handicapped artists and promoting the work of the Association. In 1988 he was elected to the Board of the Association which meant traveling to Liechtenstein twice a year for meetings with other board members from different parts of the world.

He also became a trustee for the Association's Trust Fund for the Training of Handicapped Children in the Arts. It was a project dear to his heart as it meant he was responsible for making awards to individual children with handicaps who showed potential artistic talent and to special schools. This typical generosity of spirit is remembered by many English MFPA members who were encouraged by him when they joined the Association.

Discussing his physical disability Charles once said, 'Although I am disabled, as far as possible I refuse to admit it and do not like the word though it is difficult to find a satisfactory alternative. Handicapped people generally are subject to a great deal of misplaced sympathy. When this sympathy and help is understanding and unobtrusive it is welcomed gratefully. When it is sentimental and sensational it is not.

'On the other hand I remember, when traveling in France with a friend how on one occasion the words "sentimental" and "sensational" took on a different meaning. We stopped at a lovely hotel on the upper Seine, ate a very good dinner at the end of which the proprietor came to our table and asked me how I had lost my arms. To my horror my friend answered before I could, saying that I had been a captain in the tank corps and had been blown up by a mine in Italy during the war.'

'"Very sad," commented the patron.

'"Not at all," I replied. "One has love, the beauty of nature, and there is always cognac." This inspired him to produce a bottle which he helped me to drink in the course of which he became rather sentimental. For me the result the next morning was certainly sensational!'

Charles Fowler died in 1995 but his artistic spirit lives on in the many canvases he left behind which remain a delight to those who see them.

Bruce Peardon

"One has to paint to live."

On an October night in 1916 Bruce Peardon, then age seventeen, was involved in a car crash that left him a quadriplegic. Two years earlier he had joined the Australian Navy as a junior recruit and after initial training at Perth was transferred to Flinders Naval Depot in Victoria. Then he and a friend went on leave together. The return journey to base was a long one and it meant driving through the night. Bruce drove until fatigue overtook him and then his friend took the wheel while he went to sleep across the back seat. The next thing he was aware of was lying in a hospital bed. He had no recollection of his friend dozing off, the car going out of control and the crash in which his spine was injured.

For the first three weeks in the hospital things did not seem too serious, then he had a relapse and with it came the realization that he would be paralyzed for the rest of his life. As is seen by the stories of artists in this book, each person has his or her way of coming to terms with disability. Bruce said that for the first quarter of an hour he was devastated when he was told that he would not get the use of his limbs back but, as he said, 'After that I just concentrated on getting on with life. I was lucky that I was young and young people are adaptable.'

His adaptability was proved when in Austin Hospital, Melbourne, he saw two patients hard at work painting with brushes held in their mouths – Bill Mooney and James Meath were members of the Association of Mouth and Foot Painting Artists.

'The way they painted inspired me to do the same,' he recalled. 'I had painted for a hobby and strangely enough to paint with a brush held between my teeth – apart from the problem of biting the end off from time to time – seemed a perfectly natural way to paint from the start.

We are all part of the animal kingdom and animals have a knack of adapting very quickly to changes in their condition, and so it was for me. When I could no longer use my hands I found I could write almost immediately with a pencil held between my teeth, so when it came to painting I had no difficulty in using a brush this way. It was learning the correct techniques of painting that I had to concentrate on.'

An odd thing that he found was that being left-handed he painted with a brush held in the left side of his mouth.

For the next two years he persevered at his easel and studied the effect of colors upon each other, perspective and composition until he felt confident enough to follow the example of his mouth painting friends and apply to the Association to become a student. The samples of his art he submitted were judged to be of a standard high enough for his application to be accepted.

Soon after he was enjoying the benefits of being a student a big change took place in Bruce's life. No matter how well a severely disabled person is cared for in hospital he or she tends to become institutionalized, and Bruce and some other disabled people in the hospital wanted to prove they could live in the world and that by doing so it would be cheaper for the Social Services to maintain them. They acquired a house and set up their own community which, while not unique in Australia today, was a brave pioneering project in the 'sixties.

It was lack of funds that ended the experiment but it had given Bruce a taste for independence and he had no wish to go back to an institutional life. Helped by his stipend from the Association he managed to get a house of his own where he arranged for a married couple to look after him in return for accommodation. Here he spent his time working to improve his painting as full membership of the Association was now his goal. He found it impossible to attend ordinary art classes so he worked on a program of self-instruction in which he toured galleries to familiarize himself with the work of well-known artists, and studied art books to analyze the techniques of classic painters.

During this time he evolved his own philosophy of art, saying, 'I think there is too much pretentiousness in the art world – people think one has to be a Van Gogh, or starve to death in a garret. I believe one has to paint to live, and therefore I look upon myself as a commercial painter in that if I am commissioned to do a landscape or a portrait that is exactly what I have to do.'

For the Association he painted greetings cards, his favorite theme being children in amazing situations.

In 1970 Bruce, who had been working as a student for six years, achieved his goal when he was made a full member of the Association, and soon afterwards several one-man exhibitions of his work were held. It was a very good year, but what capped it was his meeting with a nurse named Christine Halliday whom he married in 1973.

Four years later they were able to buy a plot of land set in delightful bushland seventeen miles south-west of Brisbane, and here they had their house built.

'It is very conducive to painting,' said Bruce, 'being surrounded by lovely trees and plenty of animal and bird life.'

The latter no doubt provided inspiration for 'Teddy's Night Lost in the Bush'. This was a children's book that Bruce wrote and illustrated, its story told in verse and its delight comes from the lovingly painted illustrations depicting animals of the Australian bush. In the book a teddy bear introduces young Australian readers to their wildlife heritage but it became so popular abroad that it was translated into three languages. This was followed by another Australian outback story 'Old Billy's Enchanted Valley'.

In the story old Billy replants trees in a valley that has been deforested and the wildlife – kangaroos, bandicoots, possums – return and the natural order is restored.

Bruce demonstrated his sensitivity in writing for children when, in the story, Old Billy passes away and a grandfather kangaroo speaks of death to his little grandson when he asks, 'Will you die, Grandad?'

'Yes, one day, little one, all of us die when we're old... sometimes creatures when they're young... you see, we don't really die. Our bodies may go away but all of us keep living by the memories we leave with others...'

Those words could have been Bruce's epitaph after he died in 2001.

Erich Stegmann

"No charity please."

On the wintry day of March 4, 1912 in the old German town of Darmstadt, a son was born to Alois and Olga Stegmann. The doctor told the proud father, 'Herr Stegmann, you have a fine healthy son. Do you have a name for the little fellow?' 'Yes. We decided that if we had a boy he would be called Arnulf Erich.'

In the following weeks Arnulf Erich – the family soon got into the habit of calling him by his second name – behaved as all babies should. He put on the required amount of weight and gazed with wonder about him with remarkably blue eyes. All was well with the Stegmann family which moved to Nuremberg in 1914. Then in June of that year the doctor was called to little Erich who was suddenly stricken by an agonizing illness.

'It is more than a fever,' said the doctor. 'I should like to have the opinion of a specialist in childhood ailments.'

The specialist arrived, made an examination and then told the stricken parents that their son had infantile paralysis – the only name for poliomyelitis. Some days later the actual paralysis set in and Erich's parents were told, 'He will be able to walk but not for very long distances. As for the upper limbs there can be no hope.'

The specialist was correct. When the illness passed the boy was left disabled without the use of his arms. He was constantly aware of his disability when he saw his brothers and sister playing and was powerless to join in with them.

Later, when Erich was taken to school with his useless hands tucked neatly in his pockets, he sat stiffly at the back of the class and watched his fellow pupils working with pencils and crayons in their hands. If he felt like crying with frustration he held his tears back – his mother was not there to wipe them away. Instead he managed to contrive to get the end of a pencil between his teeth and tried to form his letters with it.

'I began to write and paint with the other children,' Erich recalled later in life. 'But I wanted to do better than the others. They wrote and painted with their hands – my hands were paralyzed and I painted with my mouth so I wanted to prove to them that I could do better than those who were not handicapped. And I did it better. In fact I did so well that in 1927 I was accepted into the art school at the age of fifteen. I worked like mad and won a scholarship from the Lord Mayor of Nuremberg, where my parents now lived, to work for one year in the studio of a famous artist. The choice was left to me and I went to Erwin von Kormendy, a Hungarian painter.'

With each success Erich's confidence increased and by the time he was twenty-two he felt confident enough to leave home. He shared a studio with his brother-in-law and set about earning his living as a professional painter. The life of an artist was something he had often imagined as a boy, and now it was made all the more sweet by his relationship with a girl named Bobby Hartman who was later to become his wife. Well aware that painting, like all forms of artistic expression, is not usually a safe profession from the financial standpoint, he set up his own publishing house.

But even the art world found it impossible to ignore the politics of the 'thirties. It was a time of tension and stress, some feared the Communists and others the National Socialists led by the failed painter Adolf Hitler who, ten years after he was imprisoned for leading an unsuccessful rising in Munich, became Chancellor of Germany.

From the start Erich, with his fierce belief in individual freedom, was opposed to the Nazis and never failed to give tongue to his opposition. This, and the fact that his paintings were considered 'subversive' by the authorities, made him officially an 'enemy of the state', and as such he was arrested at the end of 1934.

For the next fifteen months he had to endure jail, not an easy situation for the able-bodied but a ghastly one for someone so physically handicapped, and as an extra piece of malice he was not allowed his paints. As a result his physical condition deteriorated so badly that the medical officer responsible for the local prison had him transferred to the Munich prison at Ettstrasse which would not be such a strain on his health. And it was at Ettstrasse that he had an unexpected birthday present – the case against him was abandoned for lack of evidence. Although he was freed he was forbidden to continue painting his 'subversive' art work, though he did continue to paint clandestinely in the countryside. Years later he became an honorary member of the board of directors of an organization representing those who had been persecuted during the Nazi period, the Vereinigung der Verfolgten des Naziregimes.

Two months after his release he married Bobby and returned to publishing greeting cards. His experience of jail did not deter him from continuing to oppose the Nazi Party and in 1944 he was forced to flee into hiding until the end of the Second World War. It was also the time when he and Bobby – with whom he shared two children – found that their marriage was not working.

In the chaos of post-war Germany Erich sought to re-establish both his professional and private life. Some time after his divorce he married Traudi Billmeir with whom he had two more children. He returned to publishing greeting 'cards', at first producing them on thin oblongs of birch wood because card and paper were unobtainable – probably the world's first wooden

postcards! He also returned to painting and in the 'fifties was having one-man exhibitions in various capital cities.

Once when told how in a Rome art gallery the proprietor made a point of telling customers Erich's pictures exhibited there had been painted by mouth, Erich exploded, 'What difference does it make how a picture is painted? A painter does not only mean a pair of hands – he paints from his heart what his eyes see. Pictures are like children who leave home. Nobody asks them whether their father has lost a foot or an arm. Why then should it arise with my pictures?'

Soon after the war Erich discovered the Adriatic island of Burano, a short boat-ride from Venice, which is noted for its traditional lace-making and colorful old-style Venetian buildings. Burano's houses with their vivid reflections trembling in the lagoon brought him back year after year. The view of him sitting in front of his easel, brush in mouth, became one of the commonplace sights of the island, and the only thing that may have struck the passers-by as odd was that he was the best-dressed artist ever to come to Venice.

In the beginning Erich painted out-of-doors as he did in his studio, in old comfortable clothing that was paint-spattered and gave off a smell of turpentine. One day when sitting at his easel to paint a street scene a crowd of instant art critics gathered round to watch and it was seen that the artist the poor fellow had to paint with his mouth! Erich had his hat on the ground beside him and to the sympathetic onlookers this meant only one thing... and coins tinkled into the hat.

Erich had to face the fact that if he sat in his comfortable, if somewhat disreputable, studio clothes well-intended coins would continue to rain on him. His solution was to wear an expensive suit, the finest shirt money could buy and a bow tie. From then on no one dared offer a coin to this personification of sartorial elegance.

Erich knew only too well the problems besetting disabled painters, and one of the main ones was the difficulty in making a living through artistic endeavor. Others, he knew had the potential to become artists but were without the means to afford training even some the cost of paints, brushes and canvases. The more he thought about this the more he became determined to establish a partnership of artists who, like himself, painted without the use of their hands – a partnership that would be commercially self-supporting. Towards this venture he sought out a small number of disabled artists who would form the nucleus of his projected organization. On March 19,1957 sixteen artists gathered for the inaugural meeting of the Association of Mouth and Foot Painting Artists in Vaduz, Liechtenstein.

'I invited you to become founder members because your work is of a standard that can be published right away,' Erich told them. 'There are others with the same problems as ourselves who have talent but need tuition to develop it. It will be the aim of the Association to seek them out and offer them scholarships so they will be provided with proper art materials and tuition until their work reaches a standard for them to become full members who will have a guaranteed income for life even if increasing disability prevents them from painting.

'The Association will be controlled only by its members but non-handicapped people will assist in the day-to-day running of it. The job of members is to paint. Arranging exhibitions and the technical side of publishing will be taken care of by those who are not disabled. After all, none of us could hang a painting or carry a set of proofs.'

Above all Erich stressed that the last thing that he wanted was for the Association to be thought of as a charity – the greeting cards and other artwork it produced must be equal, and indeed surpass, the standard of that produced by able-bodied artists. It must be bought purely on its merit, not out of pity – pity was an anathema to him. 'No charity please,' became his watchword. How successful was his vision of this artistic co-operative can be measured by the fact that today the Association has more than six hundred students and members in over sixty countries.

Despite his work as President and Founder of the Association, Erich continued with his own work. He loved to experiment with every technique possible, ranging from litho work to prints made from wood blocks he incised with mouth-held tools. And, remarkable as it may seem, he used the same method with chisels to carve wood.

Erich achieved the independent life and the reputation of a foremost artist that had been his goal as a child. Indeed, he has been described as one of the most remarkable men of the 20th century, yet as well as success he experienced tragedy – the two children of his second marriage died in road accidents five years apart.

Erich Stegmann died in 1984 but, like John Brown in the Civil War anthem, his spirit marches on. His inspiration is there every time a student or member of the Association he founded takes a brush in his or her teeth or toes and puts paint on canvas.

Marlyse Tovae

"Meaning to my life."

Early one spring morning in 1957 a meeting took place at the Wald Hotel in Vaduz, Liechtenstein. It was the first general meeting of the Association of Mouth and Foot Painting Artists which had been called by its founder and first president Erich Stegmann and was attended by sixteen disabled artists from eight European countries. Among them was a young red-haired woman named Marlyse Tovae who, like the others was excited by the thought of how the new-born Association would affect her, little dreaming of the effect she would have on the Association in the future.

The year 1957 was a good one for Marlyse. Not only had she been able to travel to Vaduz for the inauguration of the new co-operative to bring security to disabled artists, but in France she had been awarded the silver medal of the Society for Art, Science and Literature which was sponsored by the then President of France, René Coty. The honor was in recognition of her achievement as a painter despite the fact that she had been born without arms in Strasbourg in 1933.

As a young child she learned to use her feet to put on her clothing, play with toys and feed herself with the ease of able-bodied children. With such early skills going to school presented few problems but later when she was attending High School illness interrupted her studies.

One result was that while at home her interest in painting developed using pencils and paint brushes held between her toes. Her efforts were rewarded in the first year when she won first prize in an arts competition. Encouraged by this and in better health, she attended a private school run by the well known artist Marthe Kiehl, and then Strasbourg's School of Fine Arts.

When she was interviewed by the author J. H. Roesler in 1958 she told him, ' I am happy. I was always happy. I have tried to give meaning to my life and I have succeeded. I have been painting since I was eighteen. Before that I was at a school of music. Mama wanted me to become a radio broadcaster but I love painting more than anything else. The world is so beautiful and all nature is so beautifully planned, and I am just doing my little part so that people may see this.

'I have wonderful parents. The doctors advised my mother to put me in a home but Mama did not want that. She taught me to use my foot for daily things – to take up a cup, to open a door, to eat my soup with a spoon. I never missed my arms.'

One of the most thoughtful things that Marlyse's mother did was to invite neighborhood children to play in the garden so that her daughter would be used to the company of able-bodied children – and they to her – by the time she started school.

'They were all very charming to me,' Marlyse once told the author. 'Each girl wanted to be my best friend and the boys fought each other for the privilege of carrying my schoolbag.'

When she had her own home Marlyse turned it into a refuge for stray and injured animals. At one time there was a resident population of three dogs and five cats plus a fluctuating number being nursed back to health. The attractive ones were then found suitable homes, Marlyse explaining, 'It is easy to be kind to good-looking animals, the ugly and sick ones are better off with me.'

After becoming one of the founder members of the Association Marlyse continued her art career with unflagging enthusiasm. Landscapes, still life studies, portraits – all subjects were tackled and, having mobility, she was able to paint outdoors rather than copy from photographs.

A photograph in the Association's archives shows her seated in a field in Ireland painting Blarney Castle. Not only did she capture the castle on canvas but she kissed the famous Blarney Stone. This triangular stone is set high in the castle wall and is difficult to reach. To kiss it the visitor has to be held by a custodian so that half of his or her body is suspended over a dizzy drop. The reward for this hair-raising experience – so it is said – is the gift of beguiling speech. After meeting Marlyse one began to think there was truth in these old legends.

As an artist Marlyse was never content to stand still, turning to pottery, metal work and large brilliantly colored mosaics, each tiny piece being set in place with her remarkably sensitive foot. Later she experimented with abstract painting.

Erich Stegmann knew that the success of the venture depended on the artistic efforts of the first pioneering members such as Marlyse to produce greetings cards of a high professional quality to get established. And the Association benefited not only from Marlyse's painting ability but through her zest for the advancement of her fellow handicapped painters.

In 1984 Erich Stegmann died and the following year board members met to decide democratically as to who was to take over the role of president and when the vote was taken Marlyse was elected.

As president she declared, 'Today this organization allows more than two hundred mouth and foot painting artists from all corners of the globe to enjoy a secure existence. Only someone who is physically handicapped himself can judge what it means to be independent of state assistance and social welfare. For most of us this is everything, life itself and personal freedom.'

A decade after she had said this, the number of artists she quoted had doubled.

When she was in her early twenties Marlyse had said, 'I have tried to give meaning to my life.' Through her work with the Association she gave meaning to the lives of people who, like her, longed to become professional artists despite the fact they could never hold a brush in the normal way. Marlyse Tovae died in 2001 and Eros Bonamini became the third president of the Association.

North American Artists

Cindi Bernhardt
Crying Eagle, 9/11

Cindi Bernhardt
Flowers for Linda

Edward Brill
At The Lake

Edward Brill   Autumn Lake

Edward Brill Bouquet of Summer Flowers in Vase

Dennis Francesconi
Bird of Paradise

Dennis Francesconi
Bird of Paradise in Abstract

Dennis Francesconi
Mission Bell

Dennis Francesconi   A Delicate Balance

Stephen Fuller Seaworld

Stephen Fuller Valley

Michel Guillemette Le Goéland

Michel Guillemette Sailing Boat

Michel Guillemette
Old Mill

Michel Guillemette   Autumn Forest

Lynda Hamilton Still Life

Lynda Hamilton Panda Baby

Ann Harrison-May Flamingos

Ann Harrison-May Country House

Isabelle Jackson
Children in the Rain

Isabelle Jackson
Mother with a Child

Jeffrey LaDow Watermill in Winter

Overleaf:
Jeffrey LaDow
Water Lilies

Jeffrey LaDow   Bird on a White Fence

Jeffrey LaDow   Sea Life with Fish

NORTH AMERICAN ARTISTS

Daniel Laflamme Mallards in Pond

Daniel Laflamme   Fun in the Snow

Daniel Laflamme   Sunflowers

Cindi Bernhardt

"I didn't want to be an X."

A painting of the head of an American eagle with a teardrop falling from its eye was the way Cindi Bernhardt expressed her personal grief over those who died in the September 11, 2001 terrorist attack on the World Trade Center, New York.

'I painted it as a catharsis for myself and as a tribute to those who lost their lives and the public service workers who helped those in need,' Cindi explains. 'I never expected anything to come out of it.'

In fact the evocative painting became famous when it was used as the basis of a memorial insert from the American Mouth and Foot Painting Artists which appeared in The New York Times on September 10, 2002, and posters of it were presented to the emergency services in New York and Washington, DC.

Cindi's story as an artist goes back to 1981 when as a college girl she was practicing gymnastics.

'I was practicing in an open area which had a low window,' she recalls. 'I was doing backhand springs and just went backwards through the window out of control to fall two stories. I broke my neck and severed my spinal cord.

'I don't remember a thing about it which is probably a good thing.'

In the hospital, Cindi was on a respirator for three months before she was able to breathe on her own again. Then, when she was told that she would be paralyzed for life, at first she thought 'What does that mean?'

'I was a quadriplegic but I couldn't even spell the word,' Cindi told the author. 'It was devastating but I got over it just through prayer – my own faith in God and my family praying for me. There is no way I could have done it on my own. I had grown up with a faith but I was like all teenagers, you go your own way and you think you are invincible, but after my accident I had time to really contemplate a God that was a loving God. People would say to me, "Aren't you angry with God for causing this to happen?" And I'd say, "No, I believe that God did not cause this to happen, He allowed it to happen." That is a big difference, and there have been many blessings for me.

'One of the blessings was meeting my wonderful boyfriend Mike who has been a special spark in my life. He has proved that someone can love somebody who has a disability because we met after my accident. Actually, he did know me as a child as we were neighbors when I was only seven but I don't really remember him. Our meeting came about when my family went to visit his family on a Father's Day barbecue. He came over to me and said, "Love at first sight."

'I had never believed in that so I just said, "Really..." Then he said, "Well, I'd like to take you to the beach or go out with you sometime." And I thought "Oh sure, he just feels sorry for the girl in the wheelchair." But he was sincere about it and the rest is history.'

Before her accident Cindi had a very happy life with her parents and two sisters. She was the middle child and jokes, 'I consider myself the well-adjusted middle child. I say that because it is said the middle child is always trouble.' As she became enthusiastically involved in gymnastics and dance, she wanted to become a dancer. To this end she studied classical ballet but found she had started too late for a professional career, the ideal age to begin training for such a career being five. It then became her dream to have her own dance studio, a dream that ended with her spinal injury.

In hospital she thought, 'What am I going to do for the rest of my life? I have just started college and have no skills to fall back on.'

The answer came indirectly when a therapist suggested that she should learn to write with a pen held in her mouth, explaining that unless she could write her name she would have to sign legal documents with an X.

'I didn't want to be an X for the rest of my life,' says Cindi. 'So I learned how to write with a pen in my mouth, and then from writing it progressed to painting. The mother of one of the therapists would come in after hours and teach me perspective and different artistic rules and ideas. And I discovered I had a creative ability which I never knew I had before.

'I realized that artistic ability can survive within a person. Whether it is in dance form, or painting or poetry or writing, it's still artistic. So for me art became my new way of dancing.'

When Cindi's course of therapy was completed she attended Mount San Antonio Junior College in Walnut, California, where she received Associate degrees in Child Development and Mental Health and afterwards worked in helping at-risk children. But her passion for art remained as strong as ever.

'When I went back to my home in West Corvina I learned about the Mouth and Foot Artists Association,' she recalls. 'In 1991 I decided to submit some artwork which resulted with me being accepted as a student. Since then so many opportunities have come from being involved with the MFPA.'

Among these opportunities Cindi finds that the MFPA gives her the ability to share with others hope and inspiration which she does through motivational speaking at colleges, elementary schools and churches. Art comes into this as when she gives her motivational speeches she proves the value of her words by demonstrating her painting skills. As an artist she began by painting in oils but changed over to watercolor paints.

'They say it is more difficult as you can't cover up a mistake as you can in oils,' she says and adds with a laugh, 'but you learn tricks! Most of all, I like to paint people. At first I never thought I could because the proportions are very difficult but now I really enjoy portraying them – and angels. A lot of people like them and now they are one of my favorite subjects.'

One of the high points of Cindi's life came on Wednesday, January 16, 2002 when in her wheelchair she carried the Winter Olympics torch through the streets of Pasadena, California. It was part of the famous Torch Relay that bore the Olympic flame through the Games' host country to its Salt Lake City destination.

Cindi was chosen for the honor after her friend Nancy Adams nominated her because, as she says, 'They were looking for the Spirit of the Olympics and to me that is Cindi.'

The two had met when Nancy was working as a nurse's aid in a spinal cord center at Craig Hospital where Cindi was given physical therapy. It was the result of an essay that Nancy wrote about her as an 'inspirational person' that she was chosen from a great number of nominees.

Explaining her philosophy in regard to disability Cindi declares, 'I believe that acceptance is one of the most important parts in recovery. I used to think that acceptance was giving up but I have come to realize that acceptance means that you go through with it. I can't change the fact that I am paralyzed so I accept the fact that I am paralyzed. I don't like it but acceptance doesn't mean you have to like it – but you accept it and this allows you freedom to move on and allow God's work to come through your life.'

Edward Brill

"How did I do that?"

'I was a real country boy,' says Edward Brill and though as a professional artist his life has changed since his days on the farm, there is still much of the 'country boy' about him. He was born in 1961 on a farm in Cambridge, Ontario, and his earliest ambition was to become a beef farmer when he grew up. Later at High School he became fascinated by motocross racing and he financed his entry into the sport by picking tobacco leaves as a summer job. After High School he took a job at a poultry plant.

'Soon I knew that I didn't want to be a chicken plucker all my life,' Edward recalls. 'So I got further into motocross with the idea of going professional. Then I had this fluke accident. I just went over a jump the wrong way and found myself lying on the track. I tried to get up and found I couldn't. I thought I had broken my leg and that a nerve was pinched, but it turned out I had broken my neck.'

In talking about his accident, Edward does not dwell on his feelings at that time, but one can imagine what it must have been like for a young man of twenty-two who loved sports to find that in a few seconds his life had changed forever.

After an initial period in hospital, he was moved to the Lindhurst Rehabilitation Center in Toronto where he also attended the Western Technical and Community School. One day a teacher asked him if he would like to try art in order to pass the time which can hang heavy on the paralyzed.

Edward agreed to the suggestion and splints were made to which pencils could be attached. These were fitted to his hands which at that time still had a little movement. He had enjoyed drawing as a child and now he found that his attempts, though clumsy at first, re-awakened his interest in it.

After twelve months he moved to Kitchener in Ontario where the inevitable question was, 'What are you going to do for a job?' He had no answer simply because he did not know. He was paralyzed, confined to a wheelchair and all he could manage to do was some artwork as a pastime.

'Then I thought that I liked the idea of art and started looking through the phone books to get tuition,' Edward says. 'All I found there were ads for painting classes but I felt I didn't know enough about painting to go to one. I didn't want to be the stupid one in the class. Finally I saw that a guy was advertising private lessons. So I phoned him up and he turned out to be Larry Parker. He was a mouth painter and I started taking lessons with him.

'The first two pictures I did were in pencil, and Larry kept asking me why I didn't try oil paints. I wasn't very keen but he was a very persistent man and about six months later I agreed to give it a try.

'So a paint brush was stuck in the splints and I started painting an oil picture with my hand while he showed me the techniques with a brush held in his mouth. After I finished one he gave me pieces of dowel with paint brushes stuck to them and said, "When I come back next week I want you to paint with your mouth because I know you can do a better job that way."

'I thought that this was crazy, and I wasn't going to go along with it, but then I decided to give it a try and sure enough it worked. I have never looked back.'

In fact the new painting method worked so well that his artistic skill developed to such a degree, and his work was displayed in a public exhibition, the first of several solo exhibitions. His tutor

Larry Parker then introduced his work to the Association of Mouth and Foot Painting Artists, with the result he was awarded a scholarship. This encouraged him to work harder than ever, especially as in 1995 he met his partner Helen whom he had got to know through a friend after he became disabled. Two years later he became an associate member of the Association.

'It meant that we could afford to live independently,' says Edward. 'I really enjoy what I am doing and Helen helps me with my art shows and demonstrations, and she comes with me on my hunting trips. When I go fishing I often go with her brothers.'

Edward's love of the outdoors, which he enjoyed when he was 'a real country boy', has remained with him though many may wonder how a man so disabled manages to hunt and fish. He explains that when he goes fishing he uses a rod with an extension on the end so that it can be tucked under his arm which still has a slight movement although he has lost the movement in his hands for which the splints were designed. He then works the rod by leaning his body back, thus raising the rod. When he has a bite he 'pumps' the rod by moving backwards and forwards to draw the fish in.

Edward's hunting technique is somewhat different to his method of fishing because he cannot do it in his manual wheelchair. Because of the kick of the gun he hunts in his motorized chair as it has more weight to anchor him against the recoil while its arms provide stability which prevents the barrel of his gun from drooping. When hunting in his wheelchair he has to make sure he finds the right spot in the bush on level ground. Once he is satisfied with the location he shuts the wheelchair off and waits in patient silence for the game to appear.

It is not just hunting that attracts Edward into unspoiled countryside, it is there that he finds inspiration for his paintings. He explains, 'Whether I am hunting or fishing, I am out there in the bush at five o'clock in the morning and I get to see the sunrise. Then you see where all the colors are coming from. You have to actually see it to believe that Mother Nature can put those kinds of colors in the sky. People look at my paintings and say, "How did you get it like that?" But I have not painted it like that, it's just the way it is. And it changes so quickly.

'And out hunting I get the ideas for painting. If you look at a picture in a magazine you don't take that much notice but when you are out there in the real bush you really take notice and you think of things like "How did that tree ever get like that?"

'I enjoy painting so much that when I am doing it I just don't know where the time goes. But there are some days when I should not pick up the brush – it just doesn't work. But it would be wrong if it worked out right every time, and when one day it doesn't go right it makes you stop and think "What is wrong with this picture?" So you think about it, and when you go back to it the next day you say "Ah, now I know what to do."

'I love to drive my vehicle with special controls and look for scenes to paint, and sometimes it is good to get out of the house and breathe fresh air. Using oils, the paint fumes inside a room can get rather strong and sometimes you need a break from your easel.'

Apart from painting Edward visits schools to give demonstrations and show what can be done even if one is disabled. The children love to watch him at work and it gives them an understanding and respect for those less physically fortunate. He also likes to work in malls because he believes it is good to meet the public and let people see how the Association's greetings cards are painted.

No matter how many pictures Edward has produced, his enthusiasm for his work remains as bright as ever and he says, 'What fascinates me is that I can take a blank white canvas and afterwards I look at the finished product and I think, "How did I do that?"'

Dennis Francesconi

"Everything happens for a reason."

It was the sight of a child in a wheelchair pulling a small trolley behind him on which was a respirator with its tube attached to his throat that had a profound effect on Dennis Francesconi as he lay in his hospital bed.

'When I saw that I considered myself lucky,' he says. 'After all, I still had a little bit of movement and precious memories and experience of once being normal.'

A month earlier Dennis had been a very fit seventeen-year-old who loved to work on his family's ranch and was devoted to sports which included water-skiing.

'On a hot summer day in 1980 I went on a family outing to a local reservoir to have a little fun skiing,' Dennis recalls. 'I was skiing around quite quickly when the boat made a sudden turn and started heading in the other direction while leaving me on my original course. Then I realized that if I hung on to the rope I would clip a small wooden structure as well as a few rocks. So I let go of the rope and cut to the right and within mere seconds my skis made contact with the sand. I was catapulted over thirty feet in distance approximately six feet off the ground and landed on my head. I flew right past my Dad who was sitting on the tailgate of my truck. The next thing I heard following the impact was my Mom screaming.

'Oddly enough, as the bones in my neck were crushed against my spinal cord I felt no pain. In fact I didn't even feel the rest of my body hit the ground.

'Quickly I recalled that when I was younger, in two separate incidents, I had broken my wrist and my ankle and I remember that the pain of a broken bone was intense. So at that point I was expecting to simply get up. However, as I lay flat on my back looking towards the sky I soon realized that I could not move or feel anything below my shoulders. Paralysis still did not cross my mind because I knew nothing about it. Suddenly my dad appeared at my side and asked, "Are you OK?" After telling him that I could not move or feel anything he quickly instructed a friend to get an ambulance, and everyone else to stay back as he held my head steady. Obviously he knew more than I and suspected the worst.'

During the next eighteen critical days at the hospital Dennis's parents shared time there constantly. His father would sit in a chair in the corner of his room every night while his mother came during the day and did the same. That show of caring and devotion by his family, including that of his brother, is something that Dennis says he will never forget.

In the months that followed, evaluations, tests, surgeries, and the words 'permanently paralyzed' became part of his world.

Having been in hospital for slightly over three months had taken its toll. Sleepless nights and constant therapy brought pure exhaustion. On one particular night Dennis opened his eyes following a much-needed nap and through his blurred vision appeared a blue star. For a moment he was bewildered, then understood that he was looking at a television screen and the star was on the helmet of the Dallas Cowboys' quarterback, Danny White. Perhaps the star appeared as a symbol of hope – who can say? – but from then on Dennis has been an enthusiastic supporter of the Cowboys even though he has never been to Texas or seen them play a live game.

However, the realization that he was paralyzed from the chest down, and would remain so, caused him to suffer the deepest depression.

'My whole world was turned upside down,' he recalls. 'I had never been a guy who could sit down and watch television. I always had to be doing something, whether it was working, playing sports, or some sort of recreational activity. Now I had to face up to having my hands paralyzed and without feeling up to the elbows – not to mention the rest of my body. Human hands are a magnificent gift that all too often people take for granted. Look at the simple things, like petting my dog, tying my shoelace or combing my hair ... all those things were gone.'

As Dennis put it, at that point he did not consider himself lucky, but when he saw other accident patients such as those with brain injuries he thought of how he had flown through the air and hit the ground, and how easily he could have been one of them. Then, and only then, he realized that he still had something to be thankful for.

'When I went home to the ranch in Madera, California, plenty of friends would come around but I was often depressed,' he says. 'I never really let it show because I did not want to appear weak. Up until then I had loved the ranch – I was made for it, it was a perfect match, but now I found there was nothing for me to do and I hated it. It was at this point that my new best friend known as "Jack Daniels" came into the picture.'

This life of frustration continued for two years and then everything changed – this time for the better. By chance Dennis met a young woman named Kristi who he had not known prior to his accident.

In describing the effect she had on him, he has written: 'Truly a guardian angel of sorts, Kristi and I developed a relationship, a partnership, and together set out on a quest. A simplistic storybook journey it was not. Only after several long years of searching for some way to achieve and flourish did we find it.'

Kristi tried to find ways to make Dennis productive and the first thing he did was to get a real estate license as he understood farm property. With a rueful grin Dennis says, 'The only trouble was that at that time you couldn't give farm property away.'

Next he tried to sell vitamins for a company but people started looking at him as much as to say, 'You're trying to sell me vitamins? You hardly look like a picture of health.'

'Interestingly enough the breakthrough began with the need to write my name,' says Dennis. 'I had grown tired of being known as "X" so one day in an act of frustration I got a pen between my teeth and proceeded to write my name. I could not believe I had done it. So then I started writing down my thoughts and things like that, and while I wondered what to write next I would doodle. I started copying little things around the house just to kill time while I was thinking.

'Kristi started putting them on the refrigerator like I was a little kid bringing them home from school. They were 10, 20, 30-minute sketches and that's when I started thinking, "Hey, maybe I've got something." So I started doing sketches for an hour, two hours, five hours and more. I was intrigued by it and each time they got better and better.'

Dennis heard about the Association of Mouth and Foot Painting Artists through one of its older members named Clayton Turner who lived quite close to him. Clayton advised him to work more on his drawing technique before submitting anything to the Association for evaluation and also that he should use color instead of pencil or ink.

'I worked on my technique for about two years and then got in contact with the Association,' says Dennis. 'In 1993 I completed roughly a dozen pieces in watercolor, submitted them to the AMFPA and was accepted as a student right away.'

Not long after that Kristi said, 'We really should put a little more knowledge into our lives.' So she suggested that they both enroll at a local college. 'A lot of the classes we took together, the prerequisite things you have to take like English, writing, mathematics and so on,' Dennis says.

'After we completed our required classes I went on to finish my degree with art classes while Kristi was more interested in medical classes. She studied the human body, microbiology and chemistry so at times she would take me to my room, set me up to paint and then she'd be gone for another three hours doing her own work.'

Despite the demands of the college, Dennis found time to paint for the Association and in 1996 he became an associate member. In 1999 he and Kristi graduated with Associate degrees combined with full honors including membership in Phi Theta Kappa, and inclusion on the National Dean's List.

'I shall never forget our last day of college,' says Dennis. 'Just before I was due to give a farewell lecture I received a letter informing me I had become a full member of the Association. When I was wheeled into that class I felt I was about three feet off the ground.

'Membership within the Association has completely changed our lives. I had been on public support for many years which was why we were always looking for a way to be independent. Thanks to the Association I don't receive one penny from the taxpayers of this country any more. We have reversed the roles – we pay taxes now and that makes us feel good because it's the right thing to do. It was also one of our long-term goals, and we had finally achieved it. In addition, I was never comfortable surviving on the taxes of other hard working people regardless of my condition. That simply is not my style. But the most rewarding thing is to be acknowledged as an artist by an international corporation as prestigious as the Association of Mouth and Foot Painting Artists.'

Talking about his work Dennis explains, 'I mainly paint from photographs. In the past my Dad took a lot of the photos, but Kristi takes most of them now.'

Watercolor is said to be the hardest medium to use but that's what I started with and currently much of my body of work has been done in watercolor although I'm now moving to larger pieces on canvas, using either acrylics or oils.

'I like to paint landscapes, seascapes, floral pieces and I also like to do architectural studies. We live in central California, halfway between Los Angeles and San Francisco, so I try to do things within that area. I did a series of paintings of Victorian inns along the coast and really enjoyed that. I've also had the honor of seeing my work grace the covers of three national publications and one wine label thus far.'

Dennis's work is mainly representational but once in a while he enjoys experimenting with abstract or surreal pieces because it gives him the opportunity to think and paint outside of the usual lines. On average he produces between twelve and fifteen paintings a year, each taking many hours depending on its complexity. Indeed, he has been known to spend well over 150 hours on a single painting.

He is often asked if he would have ever painted if he had not had the accident to which he replies, 'I really don't know, there's no way of knowing that. I wasn't sure what I wanted to do but it would probably have been farming related because that's what we did. At school I used to admire those who could draw but in those days I could not even draw a stick man.

'As I see it, Kristi has been the catalyst in my life. If it wasn't for her, chances are I wouldn't be doing anything like this. There were things I was trying to learn for myself but she greatly enhanced my opportunities thus putting independence and success within reach. Her family has always been supportive as well. From day one they accepted me into their lives and never gave my condition a second thought.'

In 2003 one of Dennis's paintings was featured on television and had a touching sequel. It was entitled 'Freedom' and showed a section of 'Old Glory' with a soldier's dog tags hanging across it. When a friend described this painting, which she had seen in a newscast to Leslie Montemayor, she e-mailed Dennis in the hope he would sell it to her. The reason was that she found the subject very emotive as her daughter Catherine's boyfriend, PFC Diego F. Rincon was one of four U.S. soldiers who had been killed by an Iraqi suicide squad on March 29, 2003. She felt it would be a fitting tribute to the young man. Dennis explained that the picture was not for sale because he had painted it specially for his father-in-law who is a Vietnam veteran and whose name and rank appeared on the dog tags.

When Leslie Montemayor e-mailed Dennis again, he decided that under the circumstances he would find a way to re-create the 'Freedom' painting and present it to them as a gift. To do this he had the original copied twice by a local printer and during the process was able to remove his father-in-law's name and rank from the original dog tags. He then began the tedious task of changing the inscription on the tags to PFC Diego F. Rincon's name and rank. Once completed and framed he gave one picture to Catherine Montemayor and the other to Mr. and Mrs. Rincon as a tribute to their son.

'I felt compelled to do this by watching the war,' said Dennis. 'It just struck me that freedom isn't free. Sadly, in this case PFC Diego F. Rincon gave his life for freedom. Since then both Catherine Montemayor and Mr. and Mrs. Rincon have written to me and expressed their gratitude for honoring Diego in this way. It's ironic because really we should be thanking them for their son's unselfish act of bravery.'

Looking back on his life Dennis says, 'I believe God is everywhere and that everything happens for a reason. If you become disabled your senses are enhanced in another area but it is up to you to discover what that is. Maybe painting is a gift that God gave me. I think it is, and I'm truly grateful. Along the way many people have filled our lives with encouragement and praise. There are far too many to mention by name but they know who they are and to them I say "Thank you".

'Lastly, my words once again return to Kristi, my wife, my best friend and partner in life. For without her commitment, the opportunity to achieve success and total independence through the Association would have been impossible.'

Stephen Fuller

"I always liked a challenge."

To see one of Stephen Fuller's paintings of marine life beneath the waves is like looking into a brightly illuminated aquarium. Exotic fish appear to glide over colorful coral and waving clusters of sea plants while in the distance graceful dolphins perform their underwater ballets. There is a feel about the work that suggests the artist loves the subject and his aim, as he explains, 'is to help make people aware of our oceans.'

The irony is that it was underwater that Stephen met with an accident that was to alter the course of his young life.

'I was about to make a dive when a kid who was watching me yelled out, "Your feet are going to hit the rocks!"' says Stephen when describing the event. 'When I heard him I tucked my head down to look at my feet which caused me to dive deep instead of shallow.'

The impact when he struck the bottom resulted in a fracture of a cervical vertebra causing paralysis of his arms and legs.

Stephen, who had been born in Stockton, California, in 1952, was then seventeen, and for twelve months after the accident he had to remain in hospital endeavoring to come to terms with the fact that he would be wheelchair-bound for the rest of his life. The days passed with daily physiotherapy sessions and watching TV.

'I was fortunate that I got great support from my family and friends, and from my doctor,' says Stephen. 'He organized everything for me with the result that I gradually regained a little movement. When I left the hospital I could barely shrug my shoulders but five years later I did get a little movement in my arms though not enough to do much for myself or do anything like painting normally. In this case

it worked out for the best as otherwise I would not have become a mouth painting artist.'

Before his accident Stephen had no interest in art. His enthusiasm was for athletics and music which helped him in that his body was physically in good shape and this greatly assisted his medical treatment.

'I got hurt when I was seventeen so I didn't get to graduate from High School,' he explains. 'But when I was out of the hospital the High School counselor suggested I should go on to Junior College. There was a counselor at Junior College who was also a paraplegic, and he greatly encouraged me. At that time there were quite a few disabled people going to college and, as I was not the only one, I found it to be a good experience.'

Stephen did not find returning to his studies too difficult as he worked with a computer, operating it with a stick held in his mouth. And it was at this time that he learned to write with a pen held in his mouth as he had held a paintbrush.

'Learning the technique wasn't too bad as long as things were set up correctly,' he says. 'The hard part was finding a pen that would work well especially while I was at college when I had to hand in written assignments every day.'

But when his college days ended he was faced with the question that has confronted many of the people mentioned in this book – what to do with the rest of one's life?

Stephen, his brother Larry and friend Jim started a sound reinforcement and stage lighting company.

'Music had always been an important part of my life and since I couldn't play music any longer starting a sound and lighting company was a way to stay involved with music,' Stephen recalls. 'I ran most of the business end of the company. With the computer I was able to do the bookings and the book-keeping and it was a good thing I like to talk because I was on the phone a lot.'

In 1984 a friend of Stephen's named Rene coerced him into attending a painting course with her. This marked the start of his artistic career as he discovered that there was real enjoyment in painting. It was something that, despite his disability, he was in control of and it offered him a chance to express himself. His friend rented a little studio with a number of friends and working there Stephen got used to people standing behind him and watching as he put paint on his canvas. To be able to work this way was to prove to be an advantage later on when giving demonstrations.

For the next five years Stephen worked hard on improving his technique and then in 1989 a friend told him about the Association of Mouth and Foot Painting Artists. He submitted a number of his paintings for assessment and as a result was granted a scholarship. In 1997 he became an associate member.

'I always liked a challenge – when you are disabled there are plenty – but when I joined the Association I found so much was taken care of that the challenge became quite minimal,' he says. 'It is thanks to the Association that I have been able to travel to Lisbon and Vienna for members' conventions where I have met artists from all over the world who like me are disabled.'

When talking about his work Stephen, who has had numerous personal and group exhibitions, says with a grin,

'My Mom was my biggest critic – there were times she was so keen on me getting things right I had to tell her to go away. My biggest

problem with painting is that I have to recline to stay comfortable and I have to move up each time I want to get paint on my brush. This is tiring and it takes me a long time to finish a picture but I always try to get as much done as I can. And of course I am still learning.

'I use acrylic paints and I particularly like painting marine life, corals, fish, dolphins whales... I have some concerns about the environment which is one of the reasons I like painting marine life. I like to think my paintings make those who see them pay more attention to wildlife. I have visited Hawaii on a number of occasions and have a passion to live there because of the ocean and the whales.

'When my work is exhibited with that of other artists nobody knows that I paint with my mouth, and earlier on I was greatly encouraged when I won prizes at country fairs where I was up against non-handicapped artists.'

Today, Stephen lives in his own home in Stockton, California, where he is looked after by a lady named Kelley who is a long-time friend as well as a care-giver.

'I was looking for a carer so I could live on my own,' Stephen recalls. 'A friend told me about Kelley and so we met and she became instrumental in helping me to lead an independent life. Before, I got up each morning and just sat in my room, but she encouraged me to go out and overcome things that I was nervous about since my injury, like going to restaurants and baseball games. She has been with me for twenty years and her daughter has grown up with me which has been a great pleasure in my life.

'As well as painting I give talks and demonstrations at schools and colleges, and I find the kids are great. They ask more intelligent questions than adults whose first question so often is "How long does the battery of your wheelchair last?"'

Michel Guillemette

"To live an independent life."

When Canadians stuck postal stamps on their Christmas card envelopes at the end of 2000 they may have appreciated the beautifully painted nativity scene on the stamp, but few had any idea of the remarkable story that lay behind it. The stamp not only represented one of the best known events from the New Testament but to its creator Michel Guillemette it symbolized his greatest success as an artist after years of painstaking work with a mouth-held brush.

Born in Lévis, Québec in 1947 Michel enjoyed school and games like any other healthy child and in his teenage years sport became an important part of his life, especially swimming. It was on a hot July afternoon in 1966 that he and a friend decided to go swimming in the St. Lawrence River. Laughing and joking together and without a care in the world, they went to the riverbank. Michel raced forward and dived into the shimmering water – and in an instant suffered the same fate as several other artists who appear in this book.

He had not realized that the tide was so low when he dove into the deceptively bright water so that instead of gliding through it in the usual way he struck the bottom head on. The impact was enough to break his spinal column.

Unable to move, he would have drowned had not his friend waded in and brought him to the shore. An ambulance was called and he was rushed to the local hospital and then transferred for specialized treatment to the Laval Hospital. Here the nineteen-year-old learned that for the rest of his life he would be without the use of his limbs.

Christmas came and then Michel went to Sanatorium Bégin in Lac Etchemin, a long-term care facility that was geared for patients with spinal cord injuries. Here he was to remain for thirteen years. At first the days and weeks seemed endless. All he could do was listen to music and watch hour after hour of television.

He felt trapped in his own body. If only there was something he could do by himself, even if it was only to write his name. Well, he could still move his head and maybe if he held a pencil between his teeth he might manage that. He tried and although at first the pencil point made meaningless squiggles on the paper clipped to a board positioned in front of him, he persevered until letters began to form. Finally he was able to write again and he thought if he could write by this method, why not draw? At least it would help him to pass the time. As he attempted this project he not only found that it filled much of his day but that it was highly enjoyable.

In 1977 Michel decided to go to art activity classes to improve his drawing. There the supervisor suggested that he should try painting. Pencil drawings were all very well but she was sure that he would get more satisfaction from creating colorful pictures. When he looked dubious she encouraged him by telling him to try anything with a brush held in his mouth. He did try one painting, then another and became fascinated with the medium of color. He bought some painting materials and in his room started to do more and more painting. His brother encouraged him by bringing puzzle boxes for him to paint. An exciting idea was forming that art might be the key to his future, although he was well aware that he had a long way to go.

'I felt it was going to enable me to live an independent life,' Michel recalls.

In 1980 he requested to be sent to another center, the Institut de Réadaptation en Déficience Physique de Québec, an 'in-between' center to prepare disabled people to live on their own in the outside world. He stayed there six months and then moved into his own studio apartment. It was a joyful time when he moved in with the help of a carer. For thirteen years he had been used to living in institutions which, while he had been well looked after, could not give him the feeling of freedom that having his own home meant.

He continued to put in long hours of painting, always endeavoring to raise his standard and to this end he took lessons with an arts professor to improve his technique.

In 1986 he wrote to the Association of Mouth and Foot Painting Artists requesting information. In the fall of that year an executive of the Association visited him to see his work and explain that samples of it would have to be sent to the Association's head office in Liechtenstein, to be assessed by an independent panel of art experts to see if he had the potential of producing work of the same standard as that produced by average professional artists.

While Michel was waiting for the verdict on his work he applied to the government for a scholarship to study painting but this was refused. However, there was a non-profit organization that did assist him during this time. Then in 1987 the welcome news came that he had been accepted as a student member of the Association. He continued to study art and take courses and in 1995 he became an associate member.

Michel's pictures, painted in oils, take an enormous amount of time to produce because his work is so detailed. Apart from the work he does for the Association's greetings cards, his favorite subjects are landscapes and he works from photographs because of the time factor. If he spent the weeks he needed to paint in an outdoor spot the color of the trees could change. As a result of his work being presented in exhibitions his fame as an artist grew, but his most satisfactory moment came when he learned that his nativity painting had been chosen by the Canadian Post Office as one of their Christmas stamps.

Michel's work was rewarded by the Association granting him full membership in 2004.

Apart from painting Michel enjoys reading and playing chess, and he has had a happy relationship with his girlfriend Claire for many years. He first met her at the Sanatorium Bégin where she also was in a wheelchair as a result of spina bifida. She was then seventeen years old and at that time there was no question of anything but ordinary friendship. It was not until 1991 that they started going out together and their relationship began to develop.

Michel told the author, 'I am very happy with her and that is all that is important in life. She has a big room in my heart but I have not painted her portrait – even if I tried I would find her too beautiful.'

MICHEL GUILLEMETTE

Lynda Hamilton

"You see me and not my disability."

Lynda Hamilton is a lady bubbling with energy. Ask her to talk about her life and she answers briskly, 'I was born in Texas and lived there until I was twenty-one. When I was ten I had polio and became paralyzed from the neck down but I regained the use of my legs. So, during my relocation, I had the choice of learning to write with my mouth or my foot, and I chose my mouth. So henceforth I used my mouth for writing, painting and activities of that nature.'

Lynda refused to let her disability hold her back and after her schooling she went to college where she majored in psychology. At that time art had little significance for her, though as a child she had enjoyed drawing, and as she grew older this was superseded by fashion design which in turn gave way to her college studies. However, after she was awarded her psychology degree, she did start painting with a mouth-held brush as a hobby. It was just for her own pleasure and she called herself a 'closet painter'.

Her life took a significant turn when she went to California for a visit thirty years ago – and has lived there ever since.

'A very dear friend pushed me into taking my work to an art society in San Diego,' Lynda recalls. 'She insisted I meet some members and as a result I also became a member. That was the beginning of my artistic career. I began to show my work and got through that scary process of letting the public see it.'

With her devoted mother acting as a carer Lynda was able to enjoy an independent life working on her paintings and exhibiting at art shows. Then her life took another turn when she met Robert Thome, the celebrated mouth-painter whose story is included in this book, and who has been responsible for introducing a number of other disabled painters to the Association of Mouth and Foot Painting Artists.

'Several times Robert and I had exhibited at the same art shows but I had never talked to him very much,' Lynda explains. 'Then one day, when he had just returned from a conference in Vancouver, he saw my work and said, "You are doing exactly what I want." And he went on to tell me about the Association of Mouth and Foot Painting Artists and suggested I submit examples of my work to it. I thought, "What do I have to lose?"

'Encouraged by Robert I put a folio of my paintings together, sent them off and was delighted when I was accepted as a student. Now my main focus is the MFPA, though in San Diego I still exhibit locally, and I'm a member of two non-disabled artists' guilds, being a vice president of one of them – Dimensions Unlimited.'

Lynda began her painting career using oil paints but now she works mostly in acrylics which is ideal for those with a disability like hers. There is no smell of turpentine, which can be a serious irritant when the paintbrush has to be held close to the face, and there is very little clean up after a painting session. Recently she has taken to dabbling in watercolors.

'Just to challenge myself,' she explains. 'I started out painting landscapes but now my favorite subjects are children and animals – there is such an innocence and purity about them that I enjoy. I do a lot of research for my art on my computer. I can go to Paris on the Web, visit the Louvre, and if I am studying a subject I can find suitable photos. And above all I can be in contact with other artists.'

Today Lynda lives and paints in her own home.

'My mother was my attendant until she passed away recently, so I now have a wonderful lady who lives with me,' she says. 'I have helpful friends and I have my church family who are always willing to help out so I am pretty independent in my own environment. In the past I looked at my disability as a challenge and found ways to get round it, and I still do that. I look at my life and I say, "This is not working, what can I do to make it work?" I am not always objective about it but I have friends who help me to create an environment that is physically more acceptable to me.

'An example was drying my own hair. We managed to solve the problem by fixing a drier on the wall with a switch on the floor so I can turn it on with my foot. And we have removed all the round doorknobs in my home and put on little bars which I can reach up to with my foot to open the door. Thus life can be made simpler and easier by facing these challenges head on.

'I do have a dog, a wonderful Labrador who thinks she is the center of everybody's world. She's twelve now, very sweet, a good companion, and she loves you regardless. When I am painting she sits by my foot, as close as she can get.'

When Lynda was a teenager her idea of a dream car was a Mustang, and later the dream became a reality when she purchased her first car – a Mustang. This automobile was specially adapted for her by a fellow polio victim, Cameron Enns, and she found it gave her a wonderful sense of independence. Not so long ago the Mustang was stolen and was replaced by a Subaru station wagon which was also adapted by Cameron Enns. Lynda found the great advantage of the station wagon was that it enabled her to transport the work of less able MFPA artists to exhibitions.

She has a working arrangement with Robert Thome when she sometimes takes his paintings with hers to one exhibition while he takes her work to another.

Apart from that both she and Robert teach art to a class of patients at a San Diego rehabilitation center.

'They are people with various problems who come into the rehab center,' Lynda says. 'And we do some work in schools. We go into the classrooms of able-bodied children and usually Robert will paint a portrait of one of them very fast, and I work with him at the table. When they have been shown how to paint with the mouth we suggest they try it and it is fascinating to see them. "I can't do this," they say at first, but by the time they have finished they are so excited. It is a challenge but it proves to them that if you put your mind to it, you can handle it. That is my motto in life.

'These sessions are a lot of fun and they give the children an understanding of disability as well as accepting something new.'

When asked about her attitude to her work and a life which has been shaped by disability Lynda told the author,

'It has taken a few years for me to say "This is me as an artist", and I feel I am a lot closer to what I want to be as a painter though I am sure there will be more transition... I think it is inevitable in these things. But now I am not a piece of this artist and a piece of that artist – I can say this is the artist I am!

'I belong to the Church of Christ. As a child I believed in God but I did not have a lot of knowledge. I was nineteen when I became a Christian and have been blessed by the Lord throughout my life, and I have a strong Church family in San Diego.

'I have friends, some of whom have known me for years, who will reach out and try to hand me something and then say, "Sorry, I just forget." And I reply, "I'm glad you do. I'm glad that you see me and not my disability."'

Ann Harrison-May

"A God thing"

'When I was born in 1952 my parents had already experienced the death of one of my three sisters, the third-born who passed away at the age of three, five days before I arrived in this world. The doctor came into the room to tell my parents that they had a beautiful baby girl. However, she was born without arms. My Mom, heavily sedated with medications, said, "Put her back where she came from, she isn't done yet." My Dad was told to go home to rest. As he was leaving, instead of going out the front door, he entered a closet and sat for six hours, overwhelmed by the loss of one child and the disability of the new baby.

'It was the time of Thalidomide but it was not the cause of my condition as my mother had not been prescribed the drug. When I give talks to schools, little kids will ask what is wrong with me and I say "It's a God thing", and then I explain about the opportunities He has given me and how He has helped me every step of the way.'

As Ann Harrison-May developed from babyhood it seemed perfectly natural for her to use her feet and toes as other children used their hands and fingers and she says that when she started school she was 'kind of accepted but not quite'.

It was at this time, in Grand Rapids, Michigan, that Ann was fitted with artificial arms which probably drew extra attention to her disability than if she had remained without them. At first, when she started school, they were a help, but she had to make adjustments. Every few months, to her delight, the arms would break and she would miss school. Her Dad would bring art materials home, such as sketch pads, painting-by-numbers and mosaic tiling, to help her pass the time. It was not until later in life that the artificial arms were a hindrance.

Her father decided that she needed to do something more constructive and suggested that she should learn how to play golf.

'So I learned how to play golf with my artificial arms,' she says. 'But, I didn't keep on playing because my parents divorced. I graduated from High School and entered the work force up North. Although my "arms" enabled me to carry things I couldn't use them very well. For example, I was not able to feed myself. The last pair that were made for me squished me together so much I felt I could not breathe so now they're stuck in the attic of a limb shop in Florida. The only thing that I miss about them is that I used to love to ride horses, holding the reins with the hooks attached to them.'

Ann's love of art began when she was able to take art classes at Junior High School though despite her dexterity with her feet she found it difficult at first.

'I used to say, "I can't, I can't. I can't!" And my teacher would say there's no such thing as "I can't". He had faith in me and I've always remembered his words.'

After returning from the work force up North, Ann attended the Edison Community College. There she graduated with an Associate's Degree in Fine Arts, but then she found that her disability presented her with challenges which she accepted with an eagerness that marks her personality today.

Recalling her difficulties she says, 'I could not find a job because of discrimination. Employers would look at me and think, "What can she do? She doesn't have any arms so how can she manage?" They wouldn't give me a chance so I would offer to work without pay so they would see I was quite capable.

'It took me four years to get my driver's learner's permit so I drove illegal until I got my license. Then I swore I would never ride in another bus. I don't like buses because they suddenly take off before you are seated, and you can imagine what that feels like when you are unable to grab a handhold.'

With this do-it-yourself attitude Ann managed to live an independent life. After her father passed away in 1983 she moved south to Florida in 1986 for health reasons and to avoid the cold. Although she was still married to her first husband, she hoped he would join her later. However, they divorced in 1993, and a year later she fell seriously ill with pneumonia.

Looking back to that time she told the author, 'I was on life support when I had one of those "near death" experiences. I saw the white light that you hear about and I thought "I can go home now and be happy and go see my parents." I don't know whether it was some sort of dream or not, but I blinked my eyes looking at the white light and I saw my mother who looked as real as you sitting in the chair with me. I said, "You have come down to take me home..."'

In the vision Ann's mother said 'No' and told her daughter that she was not ready as there was still much ahead of her. Then she was gone as quickly as she had appeared.

'My mother passed away thirty years ago,' said Ann. 'She took very good care of me and any time I was in major trouble I felt her spirit close to me. It is something I always hold on to.'

Today Ann runs a gallery, with a partner, for disabled artists and a studio at the Lee Memorial Hospital in Fort Myers. 'It is not for foot and mouth painters,' she says, 'but people with various disabilities, victims of strokes, and geriatrics. I teach art classes in the hospital and I love that part. You get to work with the patients and help them not only in art but in their daily lives.'

'This all came about some time after I was divorced. All by myself and living on my own,

I needed something to do but I couldn't get work. When my father died he left me some money so I had four of my paintings printed up as greetings cards and started selling them from a cart on the beach. I found it too cold in the winter with the sea spray blowing in so I transferred to a flea market. One day I met my future business partner who had moved from Birmingham, Alabama, to Fort Myers and she said once she got established she would contact me. She did, and between us we opened the gallery and studio.

'My joining the Association of Mouth and Foot Painting Artists came about after I was with the studio. I had been on television in connection with it and as a result a representative of the Association came and interviewed me and I was offered a scholarship in 2002. It has turned out to be beyond my dreams, like joining a wonderful family.'

Ann met a great many fellow members at the MFPA Exhibition held in Atlanta in May 2003 where she had an unexpected challenge.

'The highlight of my trip to Atlanta was when I was able to do a demonstration for Al Gore – it was a wonderful surprise.'

Today, Ann is remarried and at her home paints in a big studio her husband fitted up for her with lots of glass windows at the back of the house.

'I paint a lot of Florida scenes, especially with palm trees that I love,' she says. 'To begin with I tried oil paints that had been given to me by my mother to encourage me but about twenty-five years ago I changed to watercolors as they are easier to carry on the brush but are a challenge to apply. I also like to do free art in which you let the watercolors run and mix. I also like pottery. I work on the wheel but because I can't reach high with my feet I make small bowls and pots.

'I feel I have had help at every step I have taken, and though I don't go to church I know God is with me always. He has given me a lot and I can't ever thank Him enough.'

Isabelle Jackson

"Thank God they accepted me."

'I don't remember it at all – it was touch and go for a while,' says Isabelle Jackson referring to the road accident in which she received severe spinal injuries. 'At first I had a hard time believing that I really was permanently paralyzed. I kept telling my doctors "I am going to walk!"'

Isabelle, a member of the Navajo people, was born in Keams Canyon, Arizona in 1955. As a girl it was her ambition to be a counselor, as she explains, 'Before my accident I really enjoyed talking to my counselors at school and I thought it would be a good thing to do.' But at the age of seventeen a hit-and-run driver ended her plans.

In the hospital she gradually began to accept the grim fact that her paralysis would remain.

'I guess I was pretty lost as to what I wanted to do with the rest of my life and I was really depressed, like there was nothing left,' she recalls.

Later she was sent to a rehabilitation center in Phoenix where she began to write letters by holding a pen in her mouth.

'I met some wonderful people there and I still go back on visits, and that's where I started thinking about school again and I thought counseling was still an open issue,' she says. 'So what I did was just go back to school. I went up to North Dakota and did two years at High School, and then I came back home.

'From writing with a pencil in my mouth I began to doodle and gradually I went on to watercolor pencils and pen and ink, and then I discovered watercolor painting. My whole life just went into it. I enjoyed it so much I didn't look for anything else.

'After I had been painting for a while I was featured in a TV magazine program called Paraplegia News. As a result I got all kinds of letters from people in my situation, and a few from members of the Association of Mouth and Foot Painting Artists telling me about the organization. At the time I did not think I was good enough to apply.'

In 1993 a friend of Isabelle's handed her a piece of paper with the address of the MFPA on it. He explained that he had found it by accident in a book and suggested that she should try it. As it turned out it was a very happy accident for Isabelle.

'I sent in some of my work and a few days later someone from the MFPA came to see me, and she told me that the Association was offering me a scholarship,' she says. 'I was very surprised but thank God they accepted me. After that I really put my whole self into my art work and six years later I became an associate member of the Association.'

Twenty years ago, when Isabelle was working on improving her artistic skills, she had to go into a nursing home for a while and there she met David, a young Scotsman, who became her husband.

'Today we live on a Navajo reservation,' Isabelle says. 'David feels at home there, in fact it was his childhood dream to live on a Navajo reservation and he loves it. He knows a little of our language, sometimes saying something in Navajo without realizing it.

'We have an eighteen-year-old son named Christopher. I had a very tough time when I was carrying him, and when I was taken to hospital he was born prematurely so he is very special. We called him God's special gift to us. Because I am in a wheelchair his father had a great deal to do with raising him.

'I come from a large family, having seven brothers and sisters, so sometimes it has seemed very quiet having just one child. Now he has joined Job Corps, an organization that educates young people and helps them to find employment.'

David finds life on the reservation very peaceful but sometimes Isabelle finds it a bit too peaceful. A problem is that it is in a desert area so the soil around her house is very sandy. This makes travel by a wheelchair difficult because the wheels sink into sand and this makes leaving the house an impossibility.

'There are times when I get cabin fever,' she admits. 'Then David takes me into town about eighty miles away and I can wheel about happily.'

Isabelle has won awards for her painting, has received distinctions, and has contributed to exhibitions in various cities across the country, as well as having had a number of one-woman exhibitions. She has been described as "predominantly painting Native American motifs".

'I tried to change but, I'm glad to say, the influence is still there,' she says. 'I sometimes paint old traditional Navajo ceremonies that we still have. I find that interesting because not too many people know about them. We sell these pictures at art shows where they are very popular.

'My Dad was a medicine man. After he retired from his ordinary work he was in great demand. Nearly everyday he was off conducting ceremonies so I have an idea of what they were. I loved listening to him telling me about them.

'Our traditions are drifting away. As each generation comes up they teach their children only English and more of the traditions are left out. I try to put them on paper, and when I am explaining them to my son I illustrate them on the materials that are used. I would like him to know his heritage and what his grandparents used to do.'

When it comes to religious faith Isabelle belongs to the Catholic Church.

'We really became involved in the church when we lived in Northern California,' she explains. 'There is a little monastery up there in the hills that we used to visit. It was the prettiest place and the monks loved Christopher. At that time he was a baby and was carried on what they call a cradle board – that's a board that Indians use to carry their babies on their backs. We became really good friends with them and still write to them.'

Isabelle particularly likes painting children and animals, and when her son Christopher was small she used him as an unwitting model for studies of children at play.

'If I saw him playing outside I would do pencil sketches of him from the window,' she says. 'I like to paint portraits and subjects for greeting cards. Children and Christmas motifs are my favorites because they are so colorful. We have a dog and a cat, and I often include the cat in my pictures. We love him, he's like a member of the family. I paint a lot, often all day, and I am working hard to become a full member of the Association.'

Jeffrey LaDow

"The painting seems to talk to me."

The boy watched fascinated as glowing colors appeared magically on the panels of a car that was gradually transformed into what he saw as a thing of beauty. His neighbors painted custom cars professionally, laying colors over colors, air-brushing to get special effects and do what they called 'transparent stuff'. It could be said that this was the beginning of Jeffrey LaDow's interest in art.

Jeffrey Allen LaDow, born in Milwaukee, WI in 1957, grew up fond of sport and anticipated that when he finished with school he would go into an auto plant like his brothers. He was particularly interested, and still is, in motorcycle and auto racing – especially vintage vehicles from the 40s and 50s – and remembers with justifiable nostalgia how he used to ride a BSA 650 Lightning.

But the joy of motorcycling, along with his other hopes and plans, suddenly ended one hot day in 1975.

'I was eighteen and it was the first day of summer with the temperature around 92 degrees when I decided to go for a swim to cool off,' he recalls. 'I dove into the water, not realizing it was only just over 5 ft deep. You wouldn't think you could break your neck in 5 ft of water but I did. It's quite a common accident.'

In hospital, Jeff lay in an intensive care unit and had what he describes as a 'touch and go time'. His lungs did not stabilize and on one occasion they actually collapsed. Twice he had to have a tracheotomy. It was only after two and a half months that he had recovered enough to have an operation to re-fuse his neck.

'At first I did not know what a spinal cord injury could lead to,' he says. 'I'd heard of Evel Knievel breaking his neck and hurting his back so many times so I thought, "Maybe I'll be in hospital for a couple months and end up walking again." I never knew it led to permanent paralysis but after I found out, I got over it. Religion helped me and I had very good friends around me.'

As with quadriplegic cases, Jeff was later moved from hospital to a rehabilitation center, and it was seeing a mouth painter at work there that gave him the idea of doing it himself. He says he was bored and needed something to do to pass the time. He began by 'painting by numbers', which was actually coloring in printed outline drawings with each space having a number indicating the color to be used. It might not be high art but it served to get Jeff familiarized with a mouth-held paintbrush.

Jeff had enjoyed art lessons in his school days and now that interest returned. Soon he wanted a greater challenge than 'paint by numbers', and what had begun as a hobby became a passion. His 'paint by numbers' set was put away and he began teaching himself to paint his own pictures on canvas. Later he decided to join an art class and in 1991 he enrolled for lessons at the Milwaukee Art Museum.

He was the only disabled student in the class and on the first day he could imagine the other students whispering, 'Hey, look – there's a guy who paints with his mouth.' He hid his mouthpiece – to which the handle of a brush can be attached – but once he realized that his fellow students had already understood his situation he felt better and soon the mouthpiece was in place. The novelty of having a student with such an unusual method of working in the class soon wore off and from then on Jeff was always at ease painting in front of others.

'My first picture took me two years to complete,' he recalls. 'I had to copy a painting of a castle which hung in the German section of the museum to learn the technique of the old masters. I had visited the museum a couple of years earlier and when I saw that particular picture I thought, "If only I could do that picture I would be satisfied as an artist." Well, I did do that picture of the castle and I was surprised at how well it turned out.

'It was my art teacher who introduced the idea of approaching the Association of Mouth and Foot Painting Artists. At first I found the idea scary, I did not think my work was good enough to submit. I sent nothing in but she kept encouraging me and after a year I thought I'd give it a try. That was in 1986 and the result was that I was accepted as a student. Believe me, it was very gratifying.'

In 2003 his untiring efforts to improve the standard of his work were rewarded when he was informed that he had been made a full member of the MFPA.

His pictures, which he paints with great concentration even for the smallest detail, have been seen by the public at various solo and group exhibitions. One of the greatest compliments to his skill came when he was commissioned to do a painting for the West Virginia State Capital's Museum.

Apart from creative work, for the past fourteen years Jeff has done a great many demonstrations at grade schools and colleges. This not only encourages the handicapped but also gives the able-bodied an insight into the disabled and what they can be capable of.

'I try to paint five days a week, at least five or six hours a day,' Jeff explains. 'Sometimes I go on and probably work for nine hours. I get into the work so deeply that the painting seems to talk to me, telling me what do next.

'I love traveling in my van and camping, though I do not drive myself,' he says. 'This way I get ideas for paintings. For example I went to Portland, Maine, and as a result have painted several pictures of the famous Portland Lighthouse. Three years ago my brother and I drove down to the Florida Keys. I went out on a boat from which everybody was scuba diving. My brother is into scuba diving as is my niece. Because I particularly like painting underwater scenes, they have given me pictures from scuba diving magazines to inspire me, and I have fish tanks at my home. When we were out in the boat I could see wonderful fish but I could also see myself down there – I think I'll be trying that next.'

If this sounds far-fetched for someone with Jeff's disability, he would point out that he has been rafting down the Colorado River and enjoys flying in sailplanes. For a more adventurous sport he is involved in parachuting. Yes, parachuting!

'I belong to the Skyknights Club and Parachuters over Forty,' he says. 'And for me it is a great summer activity. They say it can become an addiction. My brother jumps the year round and has over a thousand to his credit, and it was he who introduced me to the sport. I had seen tandem jumps done on television so when he took me to spend some time at his parachuting club I asked if I could try it. Finally they agreed.

'I was taken up to 14,000 ft with a licensed instructor who would do the jump with me in tandem. A paramedic went up to jump with us. When we left the aircraft we accelerated to a speed of 120 miles an hour. After a minute of free fall the instructor activated the parachute.

'Remember how you used to feel when you were a kid and put your hand outside the car window and let the wind bounce it around? Your whole body feels like that when you are skydiving. Being handicapped doesn't matter. Indeed, I now prefer doing two backwards somersaults out of the plane. Usually there are a couple of other skydivers who make a group with us for a minute of the free fall, and often there's a guy with a camera that stays close. After the parachute has opened and we're getting close to the ground there are people waiting to catch me when we come in to land.

'For me parachuting is always a peak experience. While I am in the air I am not disabled.'

Susie Matthias
Sleeping Dog

Susie Matthias
Carly Picking Flowers

Jean Michalski
Winter Landscape with River and Bridge

Jean Michalski   Harbor in Maine

Jean Michalski   The Dance

David Nolt
Still Life, Fruit Basket

David Nolt   The Flowers in Town

Stanley Obritski   Dee's Delight

Stanley Obritski
Flower Still Life

Stanley Obritski   Sand Dunes

Jack Reich Line Shack

Jack Reich Mustang Lake

Jack Reich
Flowers in Vase

Jack Reich   Going Home

Jimmy Rodolfos   Vaduz, Principality of Liechtenstein

Jimmy Rodolfos   Country House

Nancy Rae Litteral
Picking Daisies

Nancy Rae Litteral Tulips in Basket

NORTH AMERICAN ARTISTS

Nancy Rae Litteral   Yellow Tulips

Steven Sles
Autumn Forest

Steven Sles The Gaiety of Snow

Robert E. Smith Daisies in the Grass

Robert E. Smith Fishing Boat

Robert Thome   Dolphins

Robert Thome Running

Robert Thome
Girl

Robert Thome
Still Life with Violin

Cody Tresierra   Geese on the Pond

Overleaf:
Cody Tresierra
Winter Scene

Cody Tresierra By the Lake

Cody Tresierra Totems

NORTH AMERICAN ARTISTS

Cody Tresierra
Sunset

Cody Tresierra Lonely Skier

Brom Wikstrom
Twin Towers

Brom Wikstrom   American Harbor

Brom Wikstrom Village Cortona

Brom Wikstrom Watermill

Brom Wikstrom Mountain Lake

NORTH AMERICAN ARTISTS

Brom Wikstrom Town Living

Daniel Laflamme

"The urge for independence."

It was an anxious time for the mother of Daniel Laflamme when he arrived in the world well ahead of schedule. Like most premature babies he looked so very, very small, and this made his parents doubly concerned that he should have sufficient nourishment. Their anxiety increased over his tendency to have choking fits when he was being fed but this problem was eclipsed when a doctor had to break the news to Mr. and Mrs. Laflamme that their infant son was suffering from cerebral palsy.

Daniel was taken home where he received all the love that a baby with his handicap needed. A year later his sister Josée was born and by the time she was three years old she had become very independent. As she ran about the house Daniel watched eagerly, desperate to copy her.

He could not understand why he could not do the things that she did, like jump about or shout at the top of his voice. Instinctively Josée comprehended that her brother was not like other children and just as instinctively she became fiercely protective. A deep bond developed between them that has lasted through the years.

Daniel was eager to walk and his mother did everything she could to help him, holding him as he tried to take a step and bribing him to move forward for a cookie. The doctor had told her that there was a slight chance he might walk in the future, and when he was five years old he did in fact begin to walk without help. The eldest of four children, he was always trying to copy what the others were doing. In the family he was treated exactly as the others. He received a lot of love and this has contributed greatly to his development.

The most difficult aspect of Daniel's handicap is in the field of communication, being deaf and hardly able to speak caused him intense frustration when he tried to get his ideas across. This frustration increased when the time came for the others to go to school. How desperately he wanted to go with them, but as the family lived in a small village there was no special school for him to attend. His parents realized that if he was to have specialized help and an education he would have to leave the family environment where he felt secure. They hated the thought but nevertheless made enquiries far and wide. Finally they found what they were looking for but they could not help but wonder how their unfortunate son would manage among strangers.

Thus when he was twelve years old Daniel was taken by his parents to live in a foster home near Québec City, which would enable him to attend a special school. It was very difficult for his parents to let go of him but soon they were reassured that he was well looked after and happy in his new environment. Indeed, Daniel was lucky that with the foster family he received the same care that he had known in his own home.

He also found the special school greatly to his liking. Here he was not a disabled boy in the world of the able-bodied – he was among youngsters who were also handicapped and therefore disability was normal. Here he learned to count and the staff focused on trying to get him to communicate. Yet often when they did things for him he pushed them away because he wanted to do them for himself. This urge for independence had the effect of making him develop the use of his feet more and more.

Daniel's father worked for the Ministry of Transport and his work entailed making blueprints with a ruler and a pencil. Daniel began to imitate him by using a pencil held in his toes. Suddenly it was realized that this boy with cerebral palsy had a genuine talent for art. The recognition he received for his work engendered a growing confidence in his own talent.

When Daniel's time at the special school ended he found it difficult when he returned to his village where no one now knew him. His mother arranged for him to go to the same center – the Institut de Réadaptation en Déficience Physique de Québec – as did Michel Guillemette who also has a chapter devoted to him in this book.

The institute specialized in preparing disabled people to live on their own in the outside world. Here a dedicated social worker named Jacques concentrated on getting Daniel to integrate into society, and once he had seen Daniel's artwork he advised him to approach the Association of Mouth and Foot Painting Artists.

After Daniel's paintings had been appraised he became a student member of the MFPA in 1986, and with the help of the regular stipend from the Association he was able to go to art classes along with able-bodied students. At first he felt strange as he held his brush between his toes but this soon passed – becoming a student member meant more than a stipend, it gave him a feeling of self assurance.

After his good advice about the Association, Jacques continued to be an important person in Daniel's life. In Québec City he arranged for him to open his own bank account, taught him how to take a bus and do the things that we take for granted. As he became more independent it was no longer necessary for him to live at the center. His brother was attending the university and he moved into his apartment, and when his sister started college he went to live with her. It was good for him to stay with his brother and sister because he learned about housekeeping, which was necessary when it was considered he could move into an apartment of his own.

Once he began living alone his parents made a weekly visit to Québec City to be sure he was all right and help him with his correspondence – until he obtained a computer and learned to communicate through it. Indeed, he became so self- sufficient that he does not need the services of a carer. Today he manages to cook for himself and do all his own shopping despite not being able to use his arms. Most remarkable of all is his adapted tricycle which he can control with such hands-off skill that he frequently goes off on journeys for half a day at a time seeking scenes to paint.

Despite his disability, Daniel has good motor control of his leg and is thus able to paint with his foot. Although he works with oil paints he has developed a style in which he manages to get a pastel effect. He is particularly fond of painting studies of houses, and his sister believes that had he not been disabled he would have been an architect. She also says that through his painting he receives a lot of tenderness, and this reflects in his work.

Nancy Rae Litteral

"Disabled does not mean unable."

1954 began as the best of years for 17-year-old Nancy Rae Litteral – it felt like something out of a movie story of happy American adolescence, a prelude to a bright and exciting future. In the small Mid-West town of Wheelersburg, Ohio, she was in her last year at High School and in the fall would be going to college. Meanwhile she was an enthusiastic member of the High School Sextet, which was kept busy singing after the group had been to New York where on television they had won second place in the Ted Mack Amateur Hour.

Christian faith was an important element in Nancy's life and her only regret was that her father, who had been religious as a young man, had ceased to attend church.

Nancy says, 'I had enjoyed an ideal childhood along with an older sister, Anna Lou, and two younger brothers, Robert and David. With mother we attended the Wheelersburg Baptist Church, and Anna Lou and I were now very excited about going to the same Christian college in the fall. Our whole life was ahead of us, we felt blessed.'

This idyll was to end on the evening of May 4, 1954. It had been a warm and delightful day, and at the High School the Sextet had sung during the intermission of the Senior Class play. After the final applause Nancy was about to walk home as the family automobile was in the local garage for repairs, but friends offered to give her a ride to her house. Describing what happened next she says, 'On the way, we were hit head on by a drunken driver. The next thing I knew I was lying on the floor without movement or feeling. Later the hospital x-rays showed that my neck was broken.'

Members of Nancy's stunned family took turns to stay with her, hoping against hope that they would see her make some movement, but she remained motionless. One night her father was sitting by her bedside when she asked him to read the 23rd Psalm. He took up a Bible and, when he finished the reading with the words '...and I will dwell in the house of the Lord forever,' his daughter asked, 'Daddy, if I die will I see you in Heaven?'

It was too much for Ray Litteral. He had no answer and, unable to speak, left the room. Nancy then asked her nurse to call her pastor to tell him of the impact of her words and ask his help. As she recalled later, 'To my joy that night Daddy rededicated his life to the Lord. Our prayers were answered.'

Nine weeks after the accident Nancy's doctors had a meeting with her parents and told them that she would remain permanently paralyzed from the neck down. As there was nothing further that could be done in the hospital it was suggested that she would be better off in her home surroundings.

Although this meant that she would be back with her loving family, it was a dark period for the incapacitated girl. Looking back on that time, Nancy says, 'I went home, watched TV and cried. God hadn't answered our prayers and my life seemed ended. Instead of going off to college, here I was totally helpless with my parents taking care of me like a baby. I was full of self pity and questioning God, "Why me?"'

The mental darkness lightened when Nancy went to the Ohio State University Hospital for a year of rehabilitation, because there she met fellow quadriplegics and out of their mutual encouragement came laughter. A device designed by occupational therapists made it possible for Nancy to hold a pen in her right hand, the only part of her body below her neck in which a tiny amount of movement remained. To pass the time that can hang so heavy on the disabled, she began 'painting by numbers', putting color into outlined spaces to build up a picture.

When Nancy returned from her rehabilitation course she found inspiration in certain Bible verses, one in particular being Philippians 4:13, 'I can do all things through Christ which strengtheneth me.'

'This verse showed me that I could live a life of paralysis for the rest of my life with Christ's help,' Nancy declares. 'I was fortunate to have such dedicated parents who sacrificed so much to care for me. We settled into a daily routine. After my mother and my father got me up in my wheelchair I'd paint until my arm got tired, then I would read, type – using a mouth-held stick to hit the keys – and watch a little television before going to bed at eleven. We did this every day except Sunday when we went to church.'

Painting by numbers developed Nancy's ability to apply paint but after a while she wanted to be more creative and to this end she enrolled in a correspondence art course in 1960. She worked at this with great dedication for the next three years and she was rewarded by starting to sell her paintings.

Then she began to suffer from an arthritic disease which made it impossible to continue work with a brush fixed to her hand so she began to paint with a brush held in her mouth. One of the problems that besets mouth-painters is having to clench a brush handle between their teeth which can cause dental problems which endanger the process of mouth painting, but in Nancy's case a dentist designed a holder that protected her teeth and allowed her to paint without discomfort for hours at a time. And so that she could select different brushes without having to keep calling to her mother for help, she used brushes with magnetic handles which enabled her to change them in the mouthpiece.

As her artwork improved her favorite subjects became still life, flowers and studies of children, particularly the latter. There is a poignant relationship between the latter and a remark of hers that was quoted in a magazine article, 'What I miss the most is to take a child into my arms.'

In 1979 the Reader's Digest published an article on the Mouth and Foot Painting Artists' Association, and, as with a couple of other artists mentioned in this book, the story fired her curiosity. She submitted several of her paintings to the Association for consideration but the reply was disappointing. The board did not consider that her work qualified her for a scholarship.

Some might have been downcast by the refusal or at least dismissed it with a mental shrug, but not Nancy. At her special easel she worked harder than ever to get the pictorial effects that she wanted, and the following year she sent off another batch of paintings. This time she was accepted as a student.

In 1991 Nancy's determination and hard work was rewarded when she was made a full member of the Association, and since then people in many countries have had the pleasure of seeing her work in the form of greetings cards.

Nancy once told the author that apart from work for the Association, she accepted commissions and a large part of her earnings from these is passed on to charities and to her brother Robert, a missionary in New Guinea, to be used to translate the Bible and to sponsor children in third world countries.

'I have an art show once a year and I enter my paintings in the county fair, but most commissions come through word of mouth,' she said. 'I've painted helicopters, boats, cars, dogs and cats, and of course portraits of people's loved ones. Painting gives me much pleasure and a feeling of accomplishment. God has been good to me and blessed me with a wonderful supportive family, church and friends. I couldn't have made it without God's love or their help.

'We handicapped must not dwell on the things we cannot do, but focus on the many things we can. Disabled does not mean unable.'

If Nancy's life could be summed up in a single sentence it would be in those last five words.

NANCY RAE LITTERAL

Susie Matthias

"The value of being an artist."

It has been written of Theresa Helen Matthias – better known to her friends as 'Susie' – that she 'touches the heart of everyone she encounters'. Her conversation is punctuated by laughter and her positive attitude to life negates any thought of her being a disabled person. And to see a collection of her landscapes or studies of animals gives no hint of the years of painstaking effort it took to perfect her craft.

The sixth of nine children, Susie was born in 1962 in London, Ontario, where she still lives. She came into the world without legs or arms, her hands growing where her arms would have normally been attached to her body, and it was recognized she was a victim of Thalidomide. This was the notorious 'morning sickness' drug which at that time affected over a hundred babies in Canada.

'From about the age of three, training began to try and make me as physically independent as possible,' Susie says. 'At one stage I was fitted with artificial legs which did enable me to walk by shifting my weight from side to side, and also make me look as normal as possible. In the long run they did not work out very well. I had a fear of losing my balance on uneven surfaces – it was a real fear as I had to wear a helmet for protection – so it took a long time for me to get from A to B. I was very glad when it was decided not to continue with them.

'After the artificial limbs, it was thought that my hands might be the best way of feeding myself though of course I would be dependent on someone else cutting up the food. That didn't work, so the next thing was a sort of arm strapped to my chest by which a backwards and forwards movement was supposed to enable me to scoop food up to my mouth.' When describing this Susie breaks into laughter as she adds, 'The trouble was that it didn't quite get there.'

At that time the Educational Board had a different view of the education of the disabled from that of today, believing it was best that children with physical disabilities should be grouped together rather than go through the regular school system. Not all went to special needs schools, a group might have its own classroom in a normal school.

'I went to the Bloorview Children's Hospital School in Toronto and then the Thames Valley Children's Center in London,' Susie says. 'Early on I became interested in drawing, holding a pencil in my hand and bending over the paper to move it by means of my shoulder and side of my face. At times I had to put the pencil in my mouth to reach some areas on the paper.'

Susie's mother encouraged her daughter in this as she hoped that it would be of help to her in adult life.

Meanwhile she received vocational training to try and fit her for some sort of career.

'They wanted to see if I could answer the telephone so I might get an office job but I was too nervous and never knew what to say,' she says, again with a laugh at her past experiences. 'My mother thought I might have a career in art and I did have a job for a short time painting little ceramic pieces, being paid so much per piece.'

It was then Myron Angus came upon the scene. One of the significant figures in the history of the Canadian Association of Mouth and Foot Painting Artists, he too had been disabled from his birth in 1926, and had found fulfillment in painting, at one time having his own gallery in Toronto. Always ready to encourage those in a similar position, he heard about Susie and visited the Matthias home to see her work and was impressed by what he saw.

'At that time I was having difficulty with my hand,' Susie explains. 'Often I could not work with it properly so I had to adapt by putting the paint brush handle in my mouth so I could dab at areas I couldn't reach with my hand.'

Seeing this Myron encouraged her to use her mouth to hold her brush for all her artwork. From then on her technique improved and she spent a year taking a Fine Arts course at Fanshawe College. For several more years she received private tuition arranged by her supportive parents. The reward for this continual labor of love came in 1991 when she was invited to join the MFPA as a student and as such received a regular stipend to further her artistic career.

At last she felt she was making her way in the world. Her talent had been recognized by experts and perhaps the possibility of independence was no longer just a dream. In 1994 she went to live in a co-op housing project designed for the needs of the disabled. Here she could paint and regularly set off in her electric wheelchair to travel to the YMCA for the swimming sessions that she still enjoys.

Gliding through the water gives her a delightful sense of freedom, and swimming became her favorite way to relax away from her easel. Competing in regional games she has won several medals and ribbons in her category.

'I now swim three or four times a week for between one and two-and-a-half hours a session,' says Susie. It has been estimated that during the latter length of time she swims a total distance of a mile.

The year 2000 was one of outstanding success. In March she became an associate member of the MFPA and began to receive a monthly income in place of her student's stipend which had been for art materials and tuition. In November, Canada Post issued a special Christmas stamp reproduced from one of her paintings.

Discussing her work, Susie says, 'I paint in watercolors and tempera. I particularly like tempera because it is more opaque than watercolor. I love to paint landscapes and sea scenes. I go off with members of my family to get photographs of places that I think would make good pictures – I have to paint from photographs because it is a bit difficult for someone like me to paint from the edge of a clifftop. I am also very fond of painting animals and my long-haired Chihuahuas – mother and daughter – make very good models.

'Belonging to the Association does not just give you financial independence, what is important is the artistic side. One is thrilled that they consider your artwork is of a quality to be published, proving to yourself and others the value of being an artist and an independent person.'

Today Susie, who lives in her own apartment, is busier than ever. Apart from painting, she demonstrates her work in malls and at craft shows, gives lectures on art, manages to find time to visit her devoted family and her circle of friends – and takes part in Electric Wheelchair Floor Hockey.

'I play in the Southwestern Ontario Division, there being six divisions in the country,' she explains. 'We use a very light plastic ball and plastic hockey sticks. In my case the stick is fixed to my left hand with duck tape so I can use my shoulder to control it, which means I can only shoot from one side. My wheelchair is controlled by a joystick which I operate with my right hand. It is great fun and in the excitement of the game one forgets all about disability.'

Jean Michalski

"I try to be a good human being."

Young Jean Michalski knew all about hardship long before he became disabled. He had been born in 1936 in Vucht, Belgium, of Polish parents. His father had come to Belgium to work as a coal miner and died very young, leaving his 24-year-old widow with three children.

'We moved to Brussels and then came the German invasion,' says Jean. 'Our mother wanted us to be as safe as possible so she sent us to an orphanage far away from Brussels where we stayed until the end of the war.'

Life was grim for the children. Wartime conditions meant that food was very short and the lack of fuel meant that most of the time they were shivering from the cold. Added to this was the fact that the regime at the orphanage could only be described as harsh.

'We were very traumatized,' Jean recalls. 'We barely spoke to each other and as a result I was very shy – even now I still am a little bit. The only difference between us and the other kids was that we still had a mother who somehow managed to keep in touch with us. In Brussels she worked as a nurse in a hospital which had been taken over by the Germans. Although she was Polish she had been born in Germany and spoke German fluently which helped a lot until she was once jailed for slapping a German officer who would not take "No" for an answer. '

Jean can still remember the taste of the chocolate given to him by English soldiers when Belgium was liberated. His mother then found work as a waitress in Brussels and her children were able to be reunited with her.

One day Jean and his brother went to watch a soccer match with a gang of their friends. He still laughs when he tells how one of the boys had a whistle which he kept blowing. This interfered with the game as the players kept mistaking it for the referee's whistle so the match was stopped until the boys were ejected from the ground.

Full of high spirits the boys started showing off to each other by trying to climb a utility pole in a field. Jean was the first to start going up and was followed by a boy who was the 'little boss' of the group. Annoyed at not being first he shouted for Jean to come down, adding, 'If you don't I'll take you down.'

Jean panicked and climbed higher with the boy close behind. Then everything went black as he touched a cable and eleven thousand volts surged through him. Unconscious, he fell 45 ft to the ground. The electric flash raised the alarm and Jean was rushed to hospital.

'Gangrene set in and the doctor told me I had to have both my arms amputated at the shoulder,' Jean says. 'I was four months in the hospital and after I was able to go home my mother did her best to get me into a school. The schools refused me – it was like I had a bad disease – so after some months mother sent me to an institution in Flanders run by the Brothers of Love. It held three hundred Flemish kids and because I spoke only French I was bullied, spat on and, being without the means of saving myself, frequently tripped up. The Brothers did not like me either and were often unkind.'

Copying illustrations in magazines with a mouth-held pen became Jean's consolation but just before he left the institution his mother asked the Brother who taught art, 'Does my son have talent?'

'None at all,' he answered. 'Don't waste money on sending him to art school.'

Hurt by this Jean shouted, 'You'll hear about me one of these days.'

After Jean left the institution without regret he continued drawing which became more and more important to him. In 1956 he was fitted with artificial arms which involved a year of rehabilitation. During this time the director of the hospital offered him a job selling postcards, cigarettes and suchlike to the patients.

'I sold postcards produced by the Association of Mouth and Foot Painting Artists which then had only just come into being,' says Jean. 'Seeing them my mother wrote about me to the office in Liechtenstein. As a result Erich Stegmann, the founder of the Association, came to Belgium to visit us. After seeing my work he said, "They're all very well but you'll have to find your style and you'll have to go to art school."

'My mother told him, "We are poor. All we have is my widow's pension and my son's disability allowance. We cannot afford anything like an art course."

'"Don't worry about that," said Mr. Stegmann. "We will pay for everything."

'So I was enrolled at the Royal Academy of Fine Arts in Brussels where I worked very hard because I knew that art was my future. In 1960 I received my diploma from the Mayor of Brussels and became a full member of the Association. You can imagine the delight my mother and I felt when the first check arrived from the Association. At last I was independent and able to follow my career.'

Two years later Jean married and a baby, also named Jean, was born to the couple. But the match was not a happy one and did not last.

'My wife left me to take care of a 15-month-old baby which is difficult when you have no arms,'

Jean says. 'I had to hire someone to help and I got divorced. Then my son and I took care of each other for the next fourteen years.'

Jean's son came to America – as did Jean's brother – and in due course he invited his father to join him in California which Jean was very happy to do.

'One day I was introduced to a lady named Nancy by my brother,' Jean remembers. 'I had just arrived and did not speak English so much, though I understood a lot through having watched American movies. She kindly offered to take me to a restaurant in her Ford Fiesta. On the way the muffler fell off on the freeway – funny the little things that come back to you – but it did not spoil the evening. We saw a lot of each other and one day I asked her if she would marry me. She said she wanted to think it over, and when she had done so she said, "Yes".

'Nancy is a wonderful wife and we have been very happy. We built a house in Ivins, Utah, and we lived there for twenty-three years. Each morning Nancy helps me dress and puts on a belt to which two dog leads are attached. Then I walk our dogs who had originally been abandoned – Frank is half coyote and Sheba is half husky. It's a wonderful way to start the day, after which I get down to work.

'I paint in oils and like vibrant colors, they give depth to a painting. I love all the seasons – all those beautiful colors you can put on canvas! – and apart from landscapes I particularly like painting sea scenes and studies of flowers. Most of the time I work from photographs and Nancy has become a wonderful photographer taking pictures for me. We make a great team.

'People ask me about my religion. My answer is that I try to be a good human being. That is more important than anything.'

David Nolt

"You name it I'll paint it."

'I had no idea of what I was running into,' said David Nolt, one of the latest people to join the Association of Mouth and Foot Painting Artists. He was referring to his arrival at the Association's International Art Exhibition held in Atlanta in 2003. When David entered the Four Seasons Hotel for the week-long stay during the exhibition, he realized he was one among over sixty artists with their carers and family members from North America. For a young man from a very rural background it could have been a daunting experience but instead he found that he was in a welcoming atmosphere.

'It was amazing – like joining a family,' he says. 'Everyone was so nice.' Association artists in wheelchairs seemed to be everywhere, talking animatedly, renewing old friendships and making new ones. Here mouth and foot painting was taken for granted and what everyone found interesting in the new recruit, who had arrived with his brother and his wife, was that they were members of the Mennonite church. Mennonites are mostly farming folk who live mainly in Pennsylvania and who continue to ignore some modern innovations in favor of leading simple Christian lives according to their faith. What struck those at the Four Seasons was how naturally happy David and his two companions appeared to be.

When David was born in 1981 at Leola, Pennsylvania, it was found that he was suffering from a condition known as arthrogypoesis, one of the world's rarest diseases. Its cause is unknown but its effect upon the baby was that his arms were complete in every way except that they lacked muscles. Despite his disability David had what he describes as a normal family background. He attended an ordinary school, walking for half a mile across the fields each day with his brother and sister. There he did not experience any difficulties in learning to write. When he was small he started drawing with a pencil held in his mouth while sitting on the farmhouse floor so that forming his letters came naturally.

'I was always drawing as a kid,' he says. 'Then around 1992 I started painting, watercolors at first and then oils, and that altered my world.'

David learned about the Association of Mouth and Foot Painting Artists through the mouth painter Jack Reich whose story also appears in this book.

'He was the one that gave me information on the Association but I did not do anything about it until later,' David says. 'I was thirteen or fourteen at the time and I waited a couple of years until I had got my skills up before I submitted my work.' He was granted a scholarship in 2001. Joining the Association has given David not only financial assistance but also the incentive to keep striving to develop his artistic skills.

'My goal is to become a full member and I have been working my way towards it,' he declares. 'I put a lot of preliminary thought into my work but do not actually paint unless I have a painting ready to go. I get my materials together and do the drawings, but once I get going on the canvas I paint everyday. I am always inspired by the life around me so I wanted to learn how to translate that to something that could be shared.'

As a painter David jokes that he is 'a jack of all trades – you name it I'll paint it' by which he means that he will tackle almost any subject. In particular he likes painting still life and animals, though his painting that was on display at the Atlanta exhibition was an oil painting of a once elegant town house with flowers growing in front of it.

Although he cannot take part in physical work requiring the use of his hands, David nonetheless has an active life.

'I spend a lot of time with nature,' he says. One of his interests is photography and using a specially adapted camera he gathers ideas for scenes that he might later reproduce on canvas. His other great interest centers around his telescope as he is an avid stargazer.

In talking about his religion David explains that his faith takes its name from Menno Simons who in the 16th century became the leader of a new Protestant religious community in Holland. Then they were known as Anabaptists and believed that the teaching of Christ in the New Testament was superior to the standards of the Old Testament. They endeavored to model their lives on His example and believed in 'baptism' in which Converts consciously entered upon a commitment to Christ as Lord. In both Catholic and Protestant countries Mennonites were persecuted, and it was to escape this that the first Mennonite colony settled in Pennsylvania in 1683. Today they continue their chosen way of life as do their neighbors the Amish who are more conservative.

As David grew up on his parents' farm, one can imagine that at times it was frustrating for him being unable to join in everyday work but in other ways he has been able to contribute. In 2002 he was featured in the Lancaster Intelligencer Journal in which he explained how mouth painting has helped him to become more independent.

Stanley Obritski

"To me it was magic."

There were roars of incredulous laughter when Stanley Obritski told his friends, 'When I'm in Rome I'm going to meet the Pope.'

'Oh yeah, you and 6,000 other people from behind some iron railing,' someone said.

When Stanley saw his friends a few weeks later he said nothing but merely produced a photograph which showed him talking with His Holiness Pope John Paul II. He had attended a conference held by the Association of Mouth and Foot Painting Artists in Rome where it had been arranged that a number of the artists had an audience with the late Pope in the Vatican.

'It was the highlight of my life,' says Stanley. 'It could not have happened if it had not been for the Association as I would never have become an independent artist.'

Stanley's story of how from despair he found artistic fulfillment and security goes back to 1960.

'Before my accident I was happy, I didn't worry about anything,' he recalls. 'I quit school, got a job and was just waiting until I was old enough to get into the military without my parents' signature because they wouldn't give consent for me to join. But I never made the military.

'My birthday was November 16 and this was only May 5. That night I went out cruising with a few of my buddies in my father's beloved car – and little did he know I had it. I was coming down the Garden State Parkway when a car in front slowed and I hit the brakes. The right front wheel caught the soft shoulder and we hit a light pole. Next I remember lying by the open window and seeing lights round us and I'm saying, "I can't feel anything... I can't move." '

Thus Stanley's destiny changed in an instant. For a year he had to remain in hospital, coming to terms with the paralysis that affected him from the neck down. Understandably he suffered from depression but he had great support from his family and the hospital staff, though he was disappointed by the attitude of his friends.

'I did see them twice – and that was the end of it. But I started making friends with people much older than me, such as injured coal miners from West Virginia who taught me the wild side of life,' he remembers with a laugh. 'Even though I could not handle the cards myself I got so good at playing poker I was cleaning them out. There was some good old times there.'

Stanley's interest in drawing was first awakened when ladies from the local school of art visited the hospital in order to encourage patients to draw as a pastime.

'They used to come over and stick felt pens in my mouth and we'd start working,' he recalls. 'The first thing I did was a horse's head – I still have it in my studio at Jackson. After three years I was able to go back home where I had the most supportive parents. I could do nothing for myself and they could have had me put in an institution instead of which they devoted themselves to looking after me.'

In 1969 he read a magazine article about an artist who painted by holding a brush in his mouth and, remembering his attempts in hospital, he applied to enroll at an art school. His application was accepted and he was given a scholarship because his parents were working people. His mother in particular was determined that he should make the most of this opportunity.

'My mother made sure I did not miss a lesson,' he says. 'I remember that once there was a terrible snowstorm and I didn't want to go to the school but she said, "You're going – you've got to do something with your life." It was a white hell outside which meant I would have a problem with my wheelchair in five inches of snow but Mother plowed her way to the school. The teacher was amazed when I appeared – I was the only one who showed up'.

To begin with, Stanley was disappointed with his work which he thought was 'stiff', then a teacher said 'Why don't you try watercolor?' He had visions of very wet paint dribbling from his brush and asked, 'How am I going to control the paint the way I have to use a brush?'

'Why don't you try?' was the answer and they began by laying washes down, and building form over them. It was a revelation to the young man who says, 'I painted with watercolors like it was a natural act.'

In 1975 Stanley applied to the Association of Mouth and Foot Painting Artists and was granted a scholarship which allowed him to dedicate himself fully to painting.

He was granted full membership eight years later and this enabled him to buy a house in Jackson, New Jersey, in which he has his studio.

'I've never known an organization like it,' he says. 'A check comes in so you don't have financial worries. And thanks to the Association I have been able to travel, going to artists' conferences in London, Rome and Vienna. It is a great experience to meet other artists, disabled like myself, from all over the world. It is like being part of a great international family.

'I was fortunate enough to meet Erich Stegmann, then our President, in 1977. We were having a get-together of the North American artists and he welcomed me like I was a long lost soul and I found he knew all about my work.

'It was his idea that when you became a member you are a member for life so that you receive your income even if ill health makes it impossible to continue painting. I've had some trauma in the last couple of years, including three operations, when I didn't know whether I'd be able to move my head again, but that made no difference to the Association. Now I'm back on the scene again only I have to paint in oils.

'Over the years my spine curved so much I could not lean forward over a table anymore which prevented me from painting on a flat surface, which gave me wet-on-wet watercolor paintings. I liked to let the colors flow like magic – to me it was magic – but when I could no longer work that way I had to change to an easel and use oils.

'I love painting the ocean and coastal landscapes and of course I paint scenes for the Association's Christmas cards such as "Santa Takes a Test Ride" which shows Santa careering down a hill on a sled or "Mr. and Mrs. Frosty and Family" – sometimes my brain works like that of a child.

'Apart from my artwork I hold an amateur radio license, the highest class of amateur radio license in the States. K2CW is my call sign and when I took my test using a mouthstick I was copying Morse code at a rate of 22 words a minute.

'I am religious – a Roman Catholic – and I have this relationship with Jesus. Everything in my life has been happy – except the accident and that was not His fault, it was mine. After it happened I wanted to die – I mean I wanted to die – but I did get spiritual help. It was as though I was being told, "Look around this world, there's plenty worse off than you. Stop being sorry for yourself."'

One of Stanley's happiest moments came in 1999 when he married his wife Myrosa.

'I had never dreamed of getting married and my wife had never been married before. Both of us were wandering through this world and the next thing, we got each other. She came to work with me and when you sit with someone in a gallery for hours and talk you certainly get to know each other. Finally I asked her, "Would you like to get married?" She said, "Yes. I never thought you'd ask me."'

Janice 'Penny' Oman

"Myron at work had been the spark..."

The Canadian mouth-painter Myron Angus, whose career is included in this book, visited the Glenrose School Hospital at Edmonton on one of his tours to demonstrate to groups of people, handicapped like himself, the possibilities of overcoming some of the problems that beset the disabled. This day he encouraged his wheelchair-bound audience by showing them how he managed to perform necessary tasks during the day such as answering the telephone, how he wrote letters with a pen held in his mouth – and how he painted.

Among those watching him avidly was a girl named Janice 'Penny' Oman who, paralyzed from the neck down, felt inspired as he created a picture with a mouth-held paintbrush. Later she was to say, 'Having seen Myron paint gave me the idea I could paint too. Myron at work had been the spark...'

As a girl Penny lived with her parents in a small community in the Peace River area where she was known for her love of sports. One evening in 1970 she set out with her friends' family to go to a movie a few miles away. On the return journey a drunk driver crossed the center line of the highway with the result being a head on crash. The parents of her friends and their five-year-old son were killed outright. Penny was in the back seat with their two daughters who survived. Penny's neck was broken by the impact.

Recalling that terrible time, she says, 'Initially I was too sick to know what a broken neck really meant. For several months I did not realize that I would never walk again. It was not until a student nurse said "if" and it was through that little word "if" that I knew. My parents had not wanted to tell me the bad news. I think that was because they did not want to accept it

themselves. And it was the doctors' and nurses' place to tell me.'

The many letters and cards Penny received from her family, relatives, classmates and students from other schools encouraged her to overcome these new challenges. As there were no special schools in the area, Penny was admitted to the Glenrose School Hospital at Edmonton where she could have rehabilitation therapy and where she did her grades 10, 11 and 12.

It was during that time that Myron Angus visited the school with his message of hope and self-help for the badly disabled and as a result Penny decided to try doing artwork at the school. She found that it complemented the way she did her homework using a mouthstick and an electric typewriter, so holding a paintbrush in her mouth was not so far from typing with a stick.

Success did not come immediately. Ahead of Penny lay untold hours of practice, the gradual learning of various painting techniques and the finding of herself as an artist. Meanwhile, she had graduated from the hospital school and the question which often emphasized the plight of the disabled arose 'what to do next.'

'I was sent to another hospital with seniors, mostly sixty, eighty, ninety years old, and I was only eighteen, an obvious generation gap,' Penny says looking back on those days. 'My roommate was eighty-two years old and deaf, and while she was a wonderful lady we had very little in common. I had been in hospital all the time since my accident because there were no housing projects available. Suitable housing was not available until the mid-seventies and I was one of the first in Edmonton to be accepted into a group home that was built from the ground up for people in wheelchairs. Altogether I was in hospital for five years and then I was in a group home for eleven years.'

While she was in the group home she saw other residents going out to work in their wheelchairs and the question never left her of 'What can I do?' She felt she did not have the skills to do the work that the others were doing. The answer came when she received a greeting card that bore the work of a member of the Association of the Mouth and Foot Painting Artists. Seeing it, Penny felt this was something she could do.

She sent a sample of her artwork to the Association and received a reply requesting more paintings to be judged by the independent jury of art experts. The result was that they saw promise in her work and in 1978 Penny was accepted as a student. Now, with help from the Association, she was able to follow her artistic career with renewed enthusiasm.

Penny lived for eleven years in the group home and in 1986 she had a wonderful feeling of independence when she moved into her first apartment. At last she had a place of her own!

Later she moved into another apartment which she shares with her husband Garry.

'Garry was doing his work placement in the building I live in when we met,' Penny says. 'We met again over coffee in one of the local malls, and began dating. We were married in 1999.'

In March of the following year her dedication to painting was rewarded when she became an associate member of the Association. This gave her the opportunity to express herself in an individual style.

Penny studied at the University of Alberta and today she makes time to visit schools and hospitals in order to teach others how to develop their artistic abilities. For many years she was a member of the Provincial Committee for 'National Access Awareness Week' which aims to make society more aware of the difficulties of the disabled.

Painting remains her passion, and full membership of the Association remains her goal.

'It gives me something to strive for and I know I can do it,' she declares. She is most inspired by the wonderful landscapes of her home country. Indeed, her love for them shines forth from her canvases. She works from memory and photographs taken of particular scenes that appeal to her. Until recently, she had company when working in the form of a little Pomeranian named Colonel who would either sit on her lap or, after she got her electric wheelchair, sit beside her in her old manual one. When Colonel 'passed on to the next world', as she put it, his companionship left a gap in her life.

Speaking about her work Penny says, 'For my painting I use watercolor and oils. I feel most at ease with oils because they are easier for me to blend. One can always come back and correct something or change it whereas with watercolor it is very fast and fluid and you have to be able to go with the flow. I paint landscapes because that is something I am most familiar with, having traveled back and forth between Grand Prairie and Edmonton. I love scenery and nature, and that reflects in most of my paintings.'

Jack Reich

"A whole bunch of determination."

To look at a Jack Reich painting is like stepping into the landscape of the legendary West, indeed his pictures have been described as 'visions of the American dream'. Jack's horses appear as though they have been caught by a high-speed camera in an instant of movement instead of having been portrayed painstakingly with a mouth-held brush. Jack's landscapes have a wide-open quality which makes one conclude that the artist not only knows his countryside but loves it.

This is true. There is nothing remarkable about someone raised on a ranch having a rapport with wide-open country, what is remarkable is how he got to know it.

Jack was born in Dupree, South Dakota, in 1936, and it was found that due to a birth defect he was unable to use his arms or legs. It seemed an extra cruel quirk of fate that he was to grow up on a ranch where there is naturally an emphasis on physical activity. It is said of the bumble bee that according to aerodynamic rules it is not capable of flight but so far no one has told the bee. So it was with Jack. He might have to use a wheelchair but that was no reason he should not do things that he would have done if he had been able-bodied.

At an early age he became an outdoorsman, learning to use his mouth to help him perform everyday tasks. He learned to ride horseback, holding the reins in his teeth, and his greatest joy was riding out into the wilderness where his handicap was forgotten – a joy that has never diminished. He also learned to hunt and fish, and when he was once asked how he managed to achieve such skills he replied in his usual laconic style, 'With a whole bunch of determination.'

Like any other youngster, Jack attended the local grade school where he found he could keep up with the class by using a pen held in his mouth, and he found particular pleasure in drawing with colored pencils. When he was a freshman in High School he wanted to go beyond pencil drawing and started experimenting with paints.

'After I graduated from High School I went to the South Dakota State University where I majored in art and minored in psychology,' Jack says. 'I received my Doctorate in 1967 and went home.'

Jack was now faced with the problem of earning a living. There seemed to be few opportunities for a man without the use of his limbs, but he was soon selling advertising space for a couple of radio stations. In the course of this he met his wife Fay.

'We got married in '71, our first daughter was born in '72, the second in '77 and the third in '86,' he says.

After his marriage he and Fay ran a motel but he still managed to find time to do some painting.

'I won a couple of prizes for my painting at the state fair and I sold a few pieces of artwork off and on which was encouraging but it was nothing very serious,' Jack explains.

Apart from his hobby and business he somehow found the time – and the energy – to go into local politics and stood for mayor of Isabel, his native town. 'I was mayor of the town for about eighteen years,' he says. 'Though I am no longer mayor, I am affiliated with city government and state government, and over the years I've done things of a civic nature.'

Despite his responsibilities Jack continued to paint, depicting scenes of the West for which he is now famous.

One day he received a copy of the Reader's Digest from a friend who wrote that there was an article in it which he would find of special interest. Jack turned the pages with a mouthstick until he came to a story about the Association of Mouth and Foot Painting Artists. Intrigued he wrote to the Association and in reply received an invitation to submit samples of his artwork. These were duly posted off and in 1981 he was granted a scholarship enabling him to dedicate more time to painting.

Jack continued to work on improving his painting skills so that in 1992 he became an associate member of the MFPA and eight years later he had the great satisfaction of achieving his goal of full membership.

Talking about his work he says, 'I paint in diluted oils, that is oils diluted with linseed oil. The linseed has to be of a very good grade and I make a point of using the very best paints there are. When the paint and the linseed oil are mixed it has the texture of rich cream which is what I find best for my style of painting. I have these diluted paints put in baby food jars so that they are in easy reach of my brush when I am at my easel.

'It's natural that I like painting horses and landscapes best, but I do other things such as still life studies. In fact I paint just about anything there is though I am not so terribly proficient as a portrait painter. I seem to have trouble in sketching likenesses. But you don't have to worry too much when you are painting a likeness of a horse's face... horses don't care one way or the other. When I sold advertising and so on I didn't have the time to devote myself fully to art until years later when membership of the Association gave me financial security. The great thing about it is that it is reassuring to know you will always be independent even if ill health should make it impossible to paint for the Association.'

Tragically Jack's wife died in a road accident in 2002.

'I've been trying to put my life together ever since then,' he says.

In this, Jack had his art and his love of the high plains as consolation. Two of his children live with him so he still has a family atmosphere in his home where his pets include two dogs, canaries, some parakeets and tropical fish.

'Apart from painting I still take time out to go fishing, do a little hunting, and once in a while play cards in the afternoon,' Jack says. 'How does a guy like me go fishing? Well, I fish out of a boat and I use an 8 ft flicking stick for a rod – which is strapped to me – and a 7 reel with a return of 33 ft of line.'

He makes it sound simple but hunting is more complicated. He has a strap connected to the barrel of his shotgun, the other end of the strap is looped round his neck to act as a balance and reduce the weight of the gun. The specially adapted rifle butt then leans against his thigh instead of resting against his shoulder and he takes aim by adjusting his stance. The trigger is pulled with a cord attached to his arm.

Jimmy Rodolfos

"Love at first sight."

It is hard – almost impossible – for an able-bodied person to imagine what it must be like to be afflicted by what might be termed 'instant disability', especially in the young. One has the use of all one's faculties, a planned future ahead and so much to look forward to – then, in an instant, it all ends with paralysis caused by some unexpected accident.

Yet, as readers of this book will have discovered, there are those who have fought back against seemingly overwhelming odds. Not only have they managed to live worthwhile lives despite disability but have developed a talent, often previously unsuspected, for art. This has not only given them self-respect and a living as professional painters but their work has provided pleasure and inspiration to others.

Jimmy Rodolfos was a popular and happy-go-lucky boy in his home town of Woburn, Massachusetts, he was often referred to as the 'Son of Tony the Barber' as his father, of Greek heritage, was a downtown barber. In High School he was keen on sports, and after fifty years remains a devoted fan of the Woburn High School football team. Another of his enthusiasms was for commercial art, painting posters for the YMCA and High School activities. He held the position as president of his class in the 11th grade and was later voted in as president of the senior class despite the fact that he was in the hospital.

In 1953 life seemed pretty good to Jimmy until July 28. Then, ten days before his seventeenth birthday, he finished work as the cook in a local restaurant – 'What Greek boy doesn't cook?' he asks – and decided to cool off with a swim in Horn Pond. A body of water with several sandy beaches, Horn Pond is a family swimming place where Jimmy had bathed since he was small, often going for a dip at six in the morning. This hot, humid summer evening he ran in from the shore, made a quick shallow dive to get wet, and hit something beneath the surface. His injury was a broken neck and a severed spinal cord so that he became permanently paralyzed from the shoulders down. Doctors told his grief-stricken parents that he would be lucky if he lived for five or six years.

'The first night of my accident was spent in the local hospital, then I was taken to the St. Elizabeth Hospital in Boston where I stayed for six months,' Jimmy told the author. 'Next, for extended therapy, I was transferred to the Massachusetts Hospital School for Crippled Children where I remained for two-and-a-half years. In occupational therapy there were several young men who had spinal cord injuries like me. I saw one of them painting by holding a brush handle between his teeth and I attempted to follow his example.'

Jimmy worked hard to master the technique and became so proficient that he had art classes and private tutoring from graduates of Massachusetts colleges of art. While at the hospital school he completed his senior high year, graduating in 1955. The previous year he had met a girl named Fay White – a meeting that was to change his life and proves that there can be such a thing as love at first sight.

'I was born in Salem – the Witch City – twenty miles from Woburn where we live today,' Fay says. 'In my sophomore year at High School I transferred to Beverly High. I was then seventeen and that summer I came down with polio on August 7 which, by a strange coincidence, was Jimmy's birthday.'

The disease left her paralyzed from the chest down but she did retain mobility in her arms. Five weeks in the Salem Hospital was followed by eleven months in a rehab institution, after which she was transferred to the hospital school where she gained her High School equivalency diploma and here she met Jimmy.

To begin with, Fay was under 24-hour quarantine to ensure that she was not carrying germs that might infect the students whose ages ranged from young children to 21-year-olds. There was a facility where the new patients were quarantined consisting of a long building with an elevator in the center. On one side there were the rooms for male patients, on the other side female patients were accommodated. Fay was allotted a room next to the elevator, the room on the other side being occupied by a young man who, like her, was confined to a wheelchair.

'One of the students, who was ambulatory, welcomed me to the facility,' Fay recalls. 'When she saw the young man sitting in his wheelchair in the open doorway of his room, she said, "I want you to meet Jimmy Rodolfos. Jimmy, this is Fay White, a new patient." We nodded. I was in a flutter and could not think of anything to say. I thought, "My God, he is handsome... that dark hair, those dark eyes..."'

'It was love at first sight and we started going steady, becoming an item, as people say. The head nurse, a spinster lady, did not want to cultivate romances between the male and female patients – I guess she figured we had enough problems! So she discouraged our relationship. I think that when we met out on the campus she watched us through binoculars because it seemed as though as soon as we got together an orderly was sent to take Jimmy back to his room for any number of reasons.'

Fay left the hospital in 1955 while Jimmy stayed on for extended art tutoring, but their relationship remained as strong as ever and they married in 1957.

Prior to Jimmy's discharge from the hospital the people of Woburn raised thousands of dollars to build a room on the back of the house where he would live to accommodate him, and to buy a hospital bed and whatever equipment he needed.

After he had married Fay, in appreciation for this wonderful gift, he did a number of paintings and through the local paper invited any and all to an open day at his house to see what he had accomplished since coming home. After the pictures were hung there was one bare spot on the wall that irritated him, so he asked his mother to go down to the local department store and buy an inexpensive frame. He then did a 20-minute painting of some flowers, put it in the frame and used it to fill the offending gap. When the guests arrived, it was the one that sold immediately.

Jimmy devoted himself to his painting and in 1962 he became the first American to be given a scholarship by the Association of Mouth and Foot Painting Artists, becoming a full member in the remarkably short time of six months.

'I mouth paint mostly in oils,' explains Jimmy. 'My favorite subjects are landscapes, seascapes and still lifes. I remember how my Dad was thrilled when one of my paintings was reproduced on a greeting card in Greece where he had been a boy.'

Fay drives their high top van equipped with hand controls and together they would set out on expeditions to find scenes that would make suitable paintings.

'We used to go out on the road during the changing of the season to fall, there was so much color out there and color is Jimmy's middle name,' Fay says. 'I would take rolls and rolls of film. New England has its own unique landscape with the stone boundary walls, rolling hills, maple trees and shadows, and from these Jimmy would either put together a fantasy from several photographs or paint a specific scene.'

Apart from his paintings that have often been displayed in exhibitions, Jimmy has given lectures over the years on the work of the MFPA and his artistic colleagues.

Jimmy and Fay have been married for nearly five decades and both rejoice they are still very compatible. Their interests include visiting flea markets, antique shows and football games, collecting memorabilia related to the Dionne quintuplets, listening to music of the 'thirties and 'forties – and Boston Terriers. These dogs have been part of their lives since the owners of a pet store, for whom Jimmy had worked as a youngster, presented him with a Boston Terrier named Sheba on his return from hospital.

'When we married eighteen months later I was the "other woman" and she barely tolerated me,' says Fay. 'I kept grumbling to myself, "If we get another dog in this house it isn't going to be a Boston Terrier." But when she passed away I had fallen in love with the breed so we got a Boston puppy and we've had Bostons ever since. Our current dog was ten weeks old when he came to us, so tiny you could fit him in the palm of your hand. I felt he was so small we had to give him a name that would bolster his morale so we decided to call him Big Guy, now shortened to BG.'

Looking back on his life Jimmy stresses how grateful he is to Erich Stegmann as the founder of the Association that has published his work, giving him the independence of a professional painter. His marriage to Fay has been equally successful.

'It has worked very well for us,' says Fay. 'We have been very, very fortunate.'

'Fay is my care-giver,' Jimmy declares. 'She is my everything.'

Steven Sles

"I extol, revel, rejoice in creativity."

When Steven L. Sles was born in Jersey City, New York, in 1940 it was found that he was suffering from cerebral palsy which caused his arms and hands to remain permanently paralyzed. Since 1959 he has been confined to a wheelchair yet despite his severe physical handicap his creative output has been truly amazing. Apart from the five thousand paintings he reckons to have produced during his lifetime, he is a poet and a serious musical composer.

As a child his creative spirit soon became evident.

'When I was six years old my neurologist recommended that my parents take me to Provincetown, Massachusetts, where the warm sand and rolling sand dunes might do my body good,' Steven recalls. 'Provincetown was a slumberous little fishing village and – in addition to New York City – it was the summer art center in America. There were a variety of famous artists who had schools there with hundreds of art students sketching and painting everywhere. I was enthralled watching art works growing from blank surfaces.'

One day Steven saw a film about a disabled artist who painted by holding a brush between her toes, proving to him that drawing and painting need not be confined to the able-bodied. He felt an urge to draw and his parents bought him a sketchpad and charcoal sticks. He held one of these in his mouth and by moving his head he began his first sketches.

It was the beginning of Steven's life-long love of painting, and looking back on that beginning he says, 'Then, who would imagine that it would lead to the plethora of visual art works – some five thousand – in watercolors, oils, casein, aniline dyes, silk screen, India ink, stained glass designs, painted porcelain and tiles which have flowed from me.'

Over the years Steven's works of art have been exhibited in 42 countries.

Steven's lawyer father became the personal attorney to a European Baron and his wife living in New Jersey who at that time owned one of America's largest private art collections. The Baroness sent the little boy boxes of modern art books which he pored over until, as he said, he lived in the world of the French Impressionists.

'I had High School art classes and at the age of fifteen I was accepted by my mentor the late Hans Hofmann, founder of Abstract Impressionism, as his youngest student in his adult class in Provincetown. He told me that if Renoir and Monet could paint with brushes strapped to their arms I could certainly paint with my mouth. "But to be a great painter," he said, "You must work very hard." Which is what I have always done.'

In 1958 Steven attended the Instituro de Allende in Mexico and then went to the small Bard College in upstate New York due to its studio program.

'For my junior and senior years I studied and graduated from Swarthmore College near Philadelphia, Pennsylvania, mostly in the Oxford-tutorial honors program,' Steven explains. 'In 1959 I went through Lisbon and Brussels' museums and art galleries en route to the University of Madrid where I was enrolled in the summer program of Hispanic culture, but I left class early each day and took a taxi to the Prado Museum.

'The day after Swarthmore Graduation I had to have tendon-release surgery from sitting cross-legged for so long at my studies. That fall, following Hans Hofmann's advice – "If you want to be a painter, paint!" – I took a studio in Manhattan for six months.'

Here as well as painting he produced his first volume of poetry.

After his formal education was completed Steven began looking for work with a feeling of self-confidence. As he says, 'I never truly felt myself to be impaired. Society had projected that label upon me. I had passed the highest academic standards of our nation, and thus armed with innate self-confidence I sought employment first at Goodwill Industries in Manhattan and expected to be offered a medium-level managerial position. In fact I was offered fifty cents an hour stuffing rag dolls. I asked incredulously, "Is that all you have to offer me?" The answer was "Yes" and I left the building feeling devastated.'

Later Steven visited the vocational guidance counselor at the United Cerebral Palsy Society of New York, an organization which had been founded by his father. Here the counselor gave him a brochure produced by the Association of Mouth and Foot Painting Artists. In reply to a letter he wrote to this organization he was invited to send ten color slides showing examples of his painting, and following this he was offered full membership.

'This was not enough for me,' Steven says. 'I had my doubts which one after the other I expressed in letters to the founder A. E. Stegmann. He took the time to patiently write to me himself during the course of half a year. He responded in a very heartfelt positive way to each of my concerns. He was very convincing and there was a deep creative, spiritual and intellectual rapport between us. My father advised me to join the Association which I did in 1964.'

In the years that followed, Steven settled in Valencia, Spain, where his output of paintings and writings was remarkable. He says that in one year alone he created 1,200 art works, wrote four volumes of multilingual poetry and received awards and honors which included

becoming a Fellow of the Royal Society of Arts of Great Britain. In 1972 he met a teacher of classical ballet and two years later they married in New Jersey.

They then moved to Tucson, Arizona where Steven lives today – and here their daughter was born. Steven not only continued as eagerly as ever on his creative projects but was also involved in volunteer work, especially in rehabilitation and care of the adult cerebral palsied. He became a special advisor to President Carter and his administration on matters of the impaired through the White House Conference on Handicapped Individuals.

In 1995 Steven and his wife divorced and some years later his health deteriorated.

'Due to my very active lifestyle I had not paid enough attention to healthcare and my impairment,' Steven explains. Despite this he remains as optimistic as ever. With round-the-clock care in his own home he declares he is more focused on his studies, composing music and writing poetry.

'I delight in my teenage daughter's evolutions and I further study Hebrew,' he says. 'I compose librettos in Hebrew and English, oratorios and ensembles, still do volunteer advisory work, and I am grateful for each additional moment in my life.'

Throughout his life Steven has had a deep sense of spirituality. Speaking of his religious beliefs, he says, 'I was brought up in a conservative Jewish home. My father was president and "gabbi" – a rabbi's assistant – of the synagogue. Several times weekly, between the age of eleven and thirteen, I went from public school to Hebrew school and then my dream was to become a rabbi. I delivered my own Bar Mitzvah speech and gave a reading in Hebrew with a speech pathologist and a rabbi's son as coaches.

'Then, from 1954 to 1974, I became a Jewish agnostic and studied the world's religions and knew many multi-sectarian clerics. As I had attended Quaker-founded Swarthmore College I became interested in Quakerism. I was told however that I could not become a Quaker and remain a Jew, and as my rabbi-professor of comparative religion at Bard College wrote to me that whatever is found in other religions is contained in the Torah which combines East and West, I took heed.

'I became increasingly orthodox since 1974 when my wife became ill. I promised to seek out God and the more I did the more He made himself known to me. During the mid-1970s I became strictly kosher. I was a member of the first orthodox Tucson synagogue and then became founder member of the second orthodox synagogue in Tucson. The newly appointed Lubavitch rabbi brought the Jewish mystical "Tanya" to my house and as I began studying it I grasped it deeply. The Torah and "Tanya" form more and more the basis for music I now compose.

'The Chassidic emphasis upon the joyfulness of life and worship through dance, song, prayer, so life-affirming, speaks thoroughly to me and I understand better the unity of divinity, of all things and of all peoples. I am not strictly Chassidic, Lubavitch, Orthodox. I am an aspiring-orthodox Chassidic, modern, unconventional Jew.

'As to my philosophy of life, my art works, writings and music are its expression as are my deeds. I try to do the very best with whatever our God of blessedness gave me at birth and imparts to me throughout my life. I extol, revel, rejoice in creativity.'

Robert E. Smith

"Why didn't I just die!"

'Now that your church has presented you with this new wheelchair, what are you going to do next?' asked the journalist from the local newspaper.

'Paint!' The instant reply came out without Robert E. Smith thinking about it. The idea had been vaguely in his mind but suddenly he knew that this was something he wanted to do against all the odds. To some the idea was ridiculous, how could a paralyzed man in a nursing home, a man who had to lie in a prone position, manage to sketch, mix colors and handle paintbrushes. But there were others who thought differently...

Robert E. Smith was born in Lamont, Florida, in 1944. He enjoyed a normal education but one thing he remembers about his school days was that art held no interest for him. As a young man he worked as a roofer until one night in 1970 he was traveling on Highway 17 when he was involved in an automobile accident. When the ambulance had taken him to hospital it was found that his neck was broken causing paralysis, for which there was no cure.

From being a healthy young man with a future, Robert suddenly found himself a prisoner of his disability, unable to do any of the simplest things that had been part of his everyday life. Inwardly he thought 'Why didn't I just die!', but outwardly he still retained enough of his sunny disposition to make jokes about his plight.

'It was a big trauma,' he told the author, 'but I have always believed in God and I know I was helped spiritually. Without that I don't think I could have made it.'

While he remained in a nursing home the congregation of Robert's church provided him with an electric wheelchair and this appeared as a story in a local newspaper. It mentioned that it was Robert's ambition to paint and this was read by some art students at the Ringling School of Art and Design in Sarasota who volunteered to get him started. When they visited him they found that he could still move his head and so it might be possible for him to draw with a pencil held in his mouth.

'I found it very difficult at first,' Robert recalls. 'One day they wanted me to draw a tiger and held up a picture of one in front of me. I tried hard but I made it too small. Then one said, "It's too close. Hold it further back so he can get the perspective." They did this and I found it worked out pretty good, but when the session was over they put my tiger in the trash with the other papers.'

When one of the housekeepers came into the room to tidy up she looked into the refuse container and saw Robert's tiger.

'Your drawing is in the trash,' she exclaimed.

'I know,' said Robert. 'Let it go.'

'I'll give you twenty dollars for it,' she declared, and she did.

Probably one of the best encouragements a budding artist can have is to find that not only does someone consider his or her work pleasing enough to have on their wall – but is keen enough to pay for it.

'If she would buy my work other people might do the same,' says Robert.

From drawing, Robert moved on to painting despite the difficulty this presented for an artist who had to remain lying on his back. One day in the nursing home a doctor, who himself had a handicapped daughter, told Robert about the

Association of Mouth and Foot Painting Artists. Having explained how the organization helped disabled people who showed artistic promise he urged Robert to send samples of his work to the Association.

'I sent them a painting,' says Robert.'They wrote me back that they saw a lot of potential in my work, and that's how I joined the Association in 1982. It meant that now I could get professional instruction and I tried to get into college to take art lessons but my niece, who took care of me, went to work and did not have the time to take me each day. So I advertized in the newspaper.'

In response, a local artist gave him instruction for a short while but as she also taught art classes she could not continue. However, one gets the impression that much of the skill that Robert shows today is a result of self-teaching.

As a result of my accident my neck was affected so that I have to lie prone,' he explains. 'If I am raised up I get dizzy. When I started painting I was lying flat on a bed and today I still have to paint in a prone position looking up at the easel fixed above my head.'

Having to work this way, with the need to hold the brush in his teeth to paint upwards, emphasizes the added difficulties that he has had to overcome.

At his home in North Port, Florida, Robert likes to paint in the garage because it gives him more quiet time to concentrate on his artwork. His invaluable helper is his grandniece Dominique who, since the age of five, has been around to adjust his canvas or assist him by dabbing oil paints on the paper towels which act as his disposable palette.

'She's my closest companion, my best supporter and now my strongest critic,' he declares. In discussing his work he says he likes painting flowers and landscapes in particular, and – with the need to produce pictures suitable for greetings cards – Christmas scenes.

'It's hard to find suitable scenes – not much snow in Florida,' he jokes. 'Most of the time I work from photographs. There was a newspaper article about me in Port Charlotte and as a result a lot of people sent me photographs that they thought would be suitable subjects.'

Among the paintings that were exhibited at the Association's 2003 International Art Exhibition in Atlanta, was one of Robert's pictures of a fishing boat heading out to the open sea. There was a sense of freedom about the scene which reflects the inner freedom that he has won for himself through his art.

Robert Thome

"Not disabled when I am painting."

Through the centuries people have been fascinated by angels, a fascination that has been reflected by countless artists who have portrayed these miraculous beings in paintings, stained glass and sculpture.

One of the latest artists to undertake the portrayal of an angel is the Californian mouth painter Robert Thome. He and three able-bodied artists were each commissioned to design and sculpt an angel for the Los Angeles Ranchos Los Amigos Rehabilitation Center. Setting to work with a pen held in his teeth, Robert devised an angelic figure 6 ft high with a wingspan of 5 ft. A fiberglass cast was made from his sketches, and then the really hard work began.

It was Robert's idea that such a mystical being should shimmer, especially when floodlit, and to achieve this he planned that the angel's surface would be covered with a mosaic of tiny mirrors. To get the exact effect he wanted, he would point with a mouthstick to the exact spot where one of these mosaics – they came in ten different colors – would be glued to the fiberglass figure by his wife Kathy. The enormity of this undertaking can be gauged by the fact that each mosaic piece only measured 1/16 of an inch, and over thirty thousand of them were required. Robert and his wife spent an average of five hours a day on the project, the most their eyes could take from working with such tiny fragments of glass. Kathy joked that it was only the daily sight of the angel that kept them from expressing very forcefully the frustration generated by such a delicate and demanding process.

Frustration apart, the Thomes' angel has been a brilliant success in both senses of the word. Summing it up Robert said, 'I was meant to do this angel. I feel honored to do something three-dimensional of this size. This is monumental for me, a real high point.'

Robert's story begins back in Los Angeles in 1969 when, as a fifteen-year-old he had an accident playing American Football in High School.

'I was making a tackle and I did it incorrectly, broke two bones in my neck and was instantly paralyzed,' he explains. 'I almost died from the impact and was rushed to an emergency hospital where it took two weeks to stabilize me. Twice I got pneumonia.

'Up to that point I had been mad about athletics and was going to try and get an athletic scholarship to college, my folks not being financially able to send me at that time. I wanted to get a scholarship and take art classes, as I wanted to become a commercial artist. I'd been interested in drawing ever since I was in kindergarten where they hung my first drawing in the school hallway. I still remember my feeling of pride that day, and my Mom does too.

'Anyway, the accident ended any thought of an athletic scholarship. Once I was stabilized I was sent to a rehab hospital and it was there that I learned to use a mouthstick. After eighteen months I was able to go back to High School in my wheelchair after which I moved on to college where I attended art classes after all.'

While he had been studying Robert had plenty to occupy his mind, but when college was over he had to accept the fact that there was little to do for someone as disabled as he. At one stage his anger and frustration became so deep that he attempted suicide.

'If you are quadriplegic it's as if you're locked in a cage and there's no way out so I just dropped out of the world,' he says. 'I would occupy my days with nothing but reading and drawing which was the only thing that still meant anything to me. Then one day my Mom showed me an article in the Reader's Digest about the Association of Mouth and Foot Painting Artists. I mailed a portfolio of my work directly to the head office in Liechtenstein. In reply they said I had an interesting technique but...

'I took it hard being turned down but it did not stop me working as by then it seemed that art was my way forward. I exhibited my work in malls and local shows and exhibitions.'

It was at an exhibition that Robert met a fellow mouth painter named Jean Michalski who also appears in this book. He liked Robert's work and suggested he should send samples of it to the Association.

'I already have,' Robert said 'You should send in your latest work and I'll give you a letter of introduction,' said Jean Michalski.

Robert took his advice and this time was accepted as a student.

'Jean had said to me, "It's going to change your life" but I had no concept of what it meant,' says Robert. 'I thought that at the very best it would be a supplement to my social security income. It turned out to be so much more than that.'

In 1980 Robert married his wife Kathy, and the couple have worked as a team ever since. Talking about her marriage Kathy says, 'I worked with Robert's stepfather, in his grocery store. The first time Robert and I met, his brother suggested we all go to a Japanese restaurant. When we got there I asked Robert if he would like me to feed him. He said "Sure" and I started, but the hardest thing to do is feed a person Japanese food. In this case it landed in his lap. What an introduction!

'"Do you think you'd do better with chopsticks?" he asked, and when I did, I had no problem.

'Three weeks later Robert's stepfather got married. Robert was best man and I was maid of honor – and that was it. I had been married before and had two children but luckily they both liked him. One night my mother telephoned me and I felt like I was twelve years old again, especially as we are a Catholic family and I was the first divorcee in the family.

'"Kathy, are you sure you are in love with this man?" she asked and I was able to say, "Yes, I certainly am." My daughter Melissa was very sweet and said, "Mummy, if he makes you happy then he should be part of our family."'

'Getting married to Kathy was amazing, a life-changing thing,' says Robert.

In 2001 the MFPA made Robert a full member of the Association, and the same year he received the Governor's Trophy, the highest honor given to a Californian with a disability. Two years later when former Vice President Al Gore opened the biggest ever MFPA exhibition in the U.S.A. in Atlanta, he was presented with a portrait of himself by Robert, wearing as usual his distinctive black hat. Afterwards Robert received nationwide television coverage when he demonstrated his mouth-painting technique for CNN.

Robert's workload could be described as prolific even by the standards of able-bodied artists. It has been estimated that in the time he has been painting with the MFPA he has produced over a thousand pictures which equates to fifty a year. Many of these works have been displayed in galleries across the country, Robert having participated in more than two hundred exhibitions in the last twenty years. On top of this, he gives talks and demonstrations to young people and adults at schools, universities and charitable organizations. With the artist Lynda Hamilton, also in this book, he continues to take part in a program he inaugurated in San Diego which is designed to take art to rehabilitation centers in order to encourage potential mouth and foot painters. He is the first to admit that without Kathy's assistance it would be impossible to cope with the demands of his varied interests.

In describing what art means to him, Robert says, 'To me painting is like prayers, like meditation and I am not disabled when I am painting.'

Cody Tresierra

"Beyond my wildest dreams."

It is said that every picture tells a story, but sometimes the picture itself is part of a story. When people look at a painting by a member of the Association of Mouth and Foot Painting Artists they have little idea of what lies behind the painted canvas. Indeed they would have no idea that the artist is disabled unless it is pointed out to them. Thus when Cody Tresierra's paintings – often tranquil landscapes – are displayed at exhibitions they give no hint of the extraordinary effort that he has put in to become a professional artist.

Cody was born in Ashcroft, British Columbia, in 1960. There was nothing out of the ordinary about his upbringing and on leaving school he looked forward to undertaking a trade. He had taken a welding course but when he spoke to local welders they told him he would do better undertaking something else. Therefore, Cody began work in a lumber mill where he saw the opportunity of advancement.

Such an idea ended when Cody was involved in a motor vehicle accident. He survived but only just, as his neck was broken and his breathing had to be controlled by a respirator as it does today. In the hospital his whole living area was 6 ft by 8 ft and he had to be constantly monitored.

'I just didn't do anything for the first couple of years,' says Cody. 'I wasn't supposed to move my neck and I wasn't supposed to sit up, so I just existed. My time was filled in watching television.'

Gradually his condition improved. Although there was no question that he would remain a ventilated paraplegic, a little movement returned to his neck and he was able to sit up.

'I guess I started painting with a brush held in my mouth because in the morning they would get you up and have you doing something even if you couldn't hold your head up straight. I found I quite enjoyed it, it was better than watching television. The first paintings I did were still life studies and the pleasure of it was that at last I had found something I could do after not being able to do a single thing for myself. I guess it is hard for an able-bodied person to understand exactly what it means – you feel written off and then to find there is something you can do... marvelous!

'At that time computers were just coming out so I started to learn about using them at the same time as I was learning to paint. But finally painting became of the greatest importance to me, though I still use a computer quite a lot. Computers are a fantastic help to the disabled, especially now that the e-mail and the web have developed. It means for someone like me I can keep in regular touch with my fellow artists.'

So far Cody had regarded his painting as nothing more than a pastime, but there were others who had a high regard for his work as it developed. One was a patient in the hospital who, as a painter herself, had persuaded him to try painting and he had often watched her at work. Cody's mother took photographs of his paintings and, unknown to him, after the pictures had been developed she sent them to the Association of Mouth and Foot Painting Artists.

'When she came and told me what she had done I got mad at her,' Cody remembers with a grin. 'Although I had become very enthusiastic about painting I still saw it as just a way of passing the time in hospital. So when the Association informed me that they would take me on as a student I felt it was not for me and I wasn't going to go through with it. Then after some thought I decided I'd give it a whirl – and I've never looked back! From my start with the Association it felt good that I was painting for others rather than just myself.'

As an MFPA student, Cody was able to devote himself fully to art and tirelessly endeavored to improve his style with every picture he painted. His efforts were rewarded fourteen years later in the year 2000 when he became a full member of the Association. From then on he had financial security and in due course he bought a house just outside Vancouver where a carer came to help him each morning. He settled down to the life of a professional artist and his work was displayed in art exhibitions in British Columbia.

June 21, 2002 remains a memorable date for Cody. On that day he married his wife Elvira. She had been a nurse in the hospital where he had been a patient, and from then on they had remained in touch, their friendship developing until the time came when they decided to share their lives.

Discussing his work, Cody says, 'I paint mainly with acrylics. They do not have the smell of oil paint which can cause irritation when you have to work up close to it.

'The other advantage is that they dry much more quickly than oils. Most of the time I have some half-finished picture hanging on my bedroom wall so that I can look at it when I am in bed and think about what needs to be done to it. Then I am anxious to get up the next day to make any changes I think fit. I usually paint from photographs but I have designed a special easel which will fit on to the wheelchair so that I can do on-the-spot painting as well. The only thing that I have to worry about is the mosquitoes.

'I spend two months a year at my parents' home and there I carry on painting and give talks at grade schools. What made me very happy was being able to take my parents to Vienna when an MFPA conference was held there. I have also been to a conference in Portugal. Once, being able to travel to Europe to meet fellow artists would have been beyond my wildest dreams.'

Brom Wikstrom

"My paintings are landmarks of my development."

There can be little doubt that there is Viking blood in Brom Wikstrom's veins. Apart from the fact that his forbears came from Scandinavia, he has something of the restless spirit which led to the Vikings reaching America before Columbus.

Born in Seattle in 1953, Brom was a ten-year-old when he went on his first exciting journey. Then his father, who had been born in Ketchikan, Alaska, sent him there to meet his relatives. The boy fell in love with the country and was particularly fascinated by the totem poles he saw. That was the beginning of his interest in Native American culture.

After leaving school he became an apprentice in his father's commercial art business and also took college courses in art. But the lure of the open road would not let him be.

'I had a wanderlust,' he says. 'I traveled around as much as I could, and moved from town to town where I would work for a while as a sign painter and then move on. In those days it was safe to hop on freight trains, hitch-hike and do things like that.'

Vivid memories of his visit to Ketchikan urged him to go back to Alaska. There he got a job on a fish-processing ship where fishermen brought their catches of crab to be cooked, packed and frozen. It was tough work with long hours and Brom might not have had the opportunity to see much if a labor dispute had not broken out. This gave him time off to 'hike all around' and see the remains of the battle which took place when a Japanese force attacked the harbor, the only battle that was fought on the American mainland in the Second World War.

'When I came back from Alaska I stayed with my folks until February 1975 when a friend and I decided to go to New Orleans for Mardi Gras,' Brom says. 'It was everything we expected – Bourbon Street, jazz, bars, girls, art...

'I got a job as a sign writer and we rented a small apartment near the colleges. With hindsight I wish we had moved into the French quarter, then we would not have been next to the Mississippi.'

It was into the Mississippi that Brom dove one sultry day. He misread the depth of the river by the shore with the result that – like some others in this book – he dove into water that was too shallow and struck the bottom with a disastrous impact. Its effect was to cause permanent paralysis and for the first seven weeks after the accident he lay in a special bed in the New Orleans Charity Hospital.

It was during this period that Brom had what might be termed a mystical experience.

'I was in a bed they sort of sandwiched me into,' he says. 'It was called a circle bed and was supposed to save me from being lifted when I had to be turned. On this occasion they whipped me over in the process of turning me from lying on my stomach on to my back with the result I got loose from the straps holding me in place and fell on to the floor. I had a tracheotomy tube attached to my neck and this was wrenched out from my throat.

'That was the last thing that I remembered before I was propelled into this amazing tunnel of light. I had a feeling of motion, the sensation of a rushing wind. It was an extraordinarily vivid experience and I think about it still thirty years later. Because I was a fairly spiritual man, a believer, I had been involved in fervent prayer – and my friends were praying for me – for four or five weeks before this so that if ever I was going to be in a state of grace this would have been the time. I was prepared for death and the experience reinforced every spiritual belief I ever had. A doctor happened to be in the room when this happened. He rushed over and applied a hand pump to the incision in my throat and resuscitated me.

'When I was sort of slowing down in my experience, I heard my brother's voice exhorting me, "Come on, Brom, come on!" Once I heard that I knew I was back in my old form. But it occurred to me that the new place I almost reached was like "ever present" – how exactly to explain that I am not sure but it made living in a wheelchair easier.'

Brom was to spend a year in hospital and, like other patients in his condition, found that time passed slowly with TV watching his only occupation. As a commercial artist he had been enthusiastic about his work and now the urge to draw again became so strong that he was determined to try to draw. At first he attempted to control a pencil with splints attached to his arm but as the only movement he could make was by the slight shifting of his body his efforts failed.

'When I held a pencil in my teeth I could get some contact with the paper but it took quite a while,' he says. 'I found I could not press down hard enough so paintbrushes and watercolors were what I graduated to. My inspiration came from Japanese characters and contemporary art. I imitated them to get practice and to get used to holding the brush in my mouth. The times when I tried to paint realistically the subject would frustrate me. I now see that after "warming up" with abstract shapes my control got better.

'What did surprise me was that with a paintbrush in my mouth I could become intensely aware of color. I used to draw in monochrome with a pencil but now I developed a sense of color that I did not have before.'

It was a stressful time for Brom when he finally left the hospital. For a year he had been with people who were handicapped like him so that disability was accepted as natural. Now he was returning to the world of the able-bodied in which he would be a stranger. What worried him most was the feeling that he would be a burden on his mother and father and his younger brother. Yet when he did go home his family did everything they could to reassure him that he was not regarded as a burden, and for several years he took painting lessons from his father.

'In 1980 I took it upon myself to apply to the Association of Mouth and Foot Painting Artists,' says Brom. 'Up until then I had not felt my work was competent enough but to my delight I was awarded a scholarship five years later. What made the good news extra special was that it coincided with my first one-man show. Two years later there was another great event in my life – I met my wife Anne.'

It seems to Brom and Anne that they were destined to come together. In 1984 Anne received an invitation to work as a dental hygienist in Lugano, Italy. When she had been there for a while she suddenly had an intense but inexplicable feeling that she should go back to the United States. This conviction became so strong that she did return, became employed in a dental program at the University of Washington – and met Brom!

'It does hit you when you recognize your soul mate,' he once told the author. 'The first time we went out we talked non-stop for four hours. Then we found we had a mutual friend from many years ago and that coincidence helped to bring us together.'

In 1999 the couple celebrated their 10th wedding anniversary on a balcony overlooking Lake Lugano. Prior to their anniversary celebration, Brom concluded a month-long stay in England where he had a solo exhibition of his work displayed at the MFPA Gallery. Brom became a full member of the Association in 1992.

Since then he has received several distinctions and prizes for his paintings which have been described as 'characterized by a beautiful clarity combined with firm graphic construction and transparent colors.' He presented his paintings to the Emperor and Empress of Japan and received the famous 'Torchlight Award' at a ceremony in Taiwan.

Apart from painting, he has taken college classes in art therapy and established an arts program at the Children's Hospital in Seattle. He also continues to demonstrate his painting style in regional schools and at local arts festivals.

Brom still has attacks of wanderlust. It recently led him and Anne to New Zealand where they visited the mouth-painting artist Grant Sharman, with whom they had made friends at an MFPA conference in Vancouver B.C. some years earlier.

'All the wonderful stories we had heard of the physical beauty of New Zealand and the laid-back charm of her people were true,' said Brom. 'It was a joy to experience a place that reminded me of Seattle and the United States as it was twenty years ago, before the current hectic pace of things today.'

When Brom saw examples of Maori carvings memories returned of the totem poles that he saw four decades ago when, as a boy, he first visited Alaska.

'The distinctive forms reminded me very much of the ferocious Bookwus carvings of the Northwest Coast Indians back home, only scarier,' he said.

In discussing his work Brom explains, 'My paintings are landmarks of my development as a painter and as a person. They serve as witness to my deep belief that creative expression finds a way to come forth no matter what problems arise.'

Brom Wikstrom meeting former President George Bush

Artists Worldwide

Iwao Adachi

"The world is as kind as it is cruel."

'If you feed birds from chicks they will remain tame – sparrows or doves, all are the same,' the teacher told the third grade class. The words made an impression on young Iwao Adachi and his friends so that when they were walking home from school it was suggested they should find some sparrow chicks and rear them as pets. And there, high on an iron pylon of an electrical substation, were a number of sparrow nests. The boys thought they were too high to reach but laughing they dared Iwao to climb up and, though inwardly reluctant, the dare was something he could not refuse.

His friends watched as he climbed higher and when close to a nest he shouted down triumphantly, 'There are sparrow chicks here.' Then for Iwao everything went black.

Afterwards his friends told him that he did not actually touch the 33,000-volt high tension cable but he was engulfed in a shower of sparks and had plunged to earth head first. As he lay crumpled on the ground they believed he was dead.

Iwao Adachi was born in 1939 in Osaka, Japan, where he lived happily with his family until their house was burnt down in an air raid. The family then moved to the home of his aunt from where he went to school which he enjoyed.

When he finally recovered consciousness after his fall from the pylon, the first thing he became aware of were the faces of his mother and father staring down at him. Behind them were crowded hospital doctors, policemen and journalists.

'Doctors said it was a miracle that I survived,' Iwao says today. 'The electric current ran through my body from my right hand and created a hole in my abdomen the size of my fist while my head was injured as a result of the fall. And all my body was burned black.' His right hand was amputated and then in two more operations he lost his right arm from the shoulder and his left from the elbow.

When he was discharged four months later his homecoming was not the joyous occasion one might have expected.

'It was miserable because it was as though I was a piece of wood,' he says. 'My mother burst into tears and my father looked away from me and kept silent. I was unable to go to school, I could not dress or feed myself – I could not live for a single day without my mother's help.'

A year later a second tragedy struck the eleven-year-old boy. His mother, on whom he was so dependent, died of a heart attack. She had suffered from a heart condition and it was believed that her son's dreadful accident had aggravated it.

Shortly afterwards his father's work called him away and boy was left alone in his aunt's house.

'She was a hard person and did not help me as my mother had,' he says. 'I remember one day how I struggled to put on my trousers by myself. I was lying on the floor, trying to work my way into them, when my friends dropped in to see me on their way to school.

'"What are you doing like that?" they demanded.

'It was obvious but I was ashamed. They left and I re-started work on my trousers. After two hours I had worked them up on to my hips but I could not manage the hook as my mouth could not reach it. Tears of vexation filled my eyes. My aunt was in the next room but she did not help me. Then by pressing against the corner of a desk and using what remained of my left arm, I managed to fix the hook. My joy at this achievement was but a passing moment. There came the need to go to the toilet and I found that to undo the hook was as hard as it had been to fix it. At the last moment I rushed into the water closet. There the thought of having to struggle to get my trousers up again made me want to cry. I just wanted to sit there forever...

'After a while one of my friends visited me on the way back from school and found me standing in my underpants.

'"What's the matter with you?" he asked. "You are still as you were. What have you done the whole day?"

'"I tried to put on my trousers..." Then I could find no more words.'

The humiliation the boy felt at not being able to look after himself had the effect of making him strive to be independent. The result was that he taught himself to do many of the everyday things of life, even needlework and drawing by using his mouth. This was inspired by his father once telling him the story of Junkyo Ohishi which he had never forgotten.

One of the most remarkable mouth painters, Junkyo Ohishi died in 1968 at the age of eighty having spent many years of her life as a third-rank Buddhist priestess in the temple district of Bukoin in Kyoto. She had lost her hands when she was seventeen when, in a fit of insanity, her stepfather attacked those about him with a sword. Later she said, 'One day I saw a small bird feeding its youngster with its beak. That was what prompted me to learn to draw with my mouth.'

A member of the Association of Mouth and Foot Painting Artists, Junkyo became famous in Japan for her Buddhist compassion and she opened a home offering sheltered accommodation for handicapped children.

Following the example of Junkyo, Iwao turned to drawing whenever he felt distressed.

'In the year that my mother passed away I began to draw pictures,' he recalls. 'It was to release my sorrow and to practice the use of mouth. At first I tried to draw straight lines, triangles or squares – it took me a year to be able to draw straight lines. After that I started to draw rough sketches and then I began using watercolors.

'I could get over my grief while I was drawing pictures, I could forget my life without arms.' Nevertheless he suffered from deep depression when not working on the scraps of paper he saved.

'I hated to be called Daruma – man without hands – and have stones thrown at me, so I exercised secretly at night,' he said. 'This later bore fruit when in the Paraplegic Games held at Yoyogi, Tokyo, I won the gold medal in the 50 meter breaststroke and a bronze medal in the standing broad jump. People said it was great – maybe, but the work that had led up to it was for surviving.'

After this Iwao moved to his father's apartment room which was vacant most of the time and he found it necessary to earn money to support himself. To this end he tried a variety of jobs, from baby-sitting to cleaning a cinema.

'People were unwilling to employ me because I did not have arms and often I worked without payment to prove that I was capable of doing a job,' he says. 'And I was thankful if someone gave me work but once I was hired I was always anxious in case I was fired – I often was and ran back home with abuse shouted after me. At one stage, when I was seventeen years old, it seemed that everything was too hard to bear and I decided I could not go on. I stood on a railway track and waited while the train came towards me with a deafening roar. At the last moment some instinct made me leap to one side.'

Two years later Iwao found regular work with the Izumiya Industries Company which manufactured road-making equipment. Having taught himself to ride a bicycle 'no hands' he was employed as a messenger at a fraction of what an able-bodied worker would earn but he was delighted to be employed.

IWAO ADACHI

It was now his ambition to try painting in oils and on April 24, 1962 – a date that is fixed in his memory – he was able to buy a set of oil colors with the money that he had saved at the rate of five yen a day. As there was not enough money for him to buy a palette he solved the problem by using the glass which he removed from his window after putting on all his clothing against the freezing cold of the winter nights.

In November of the same year Iwao entered an oil painting for showing in a Fuse City exhibition and it was not only accepted but sold for the seemingly astronomical sum of 6,000 yen.

'The success overpaid me for all my efforts,' Iwao recalls. 'I wanted to throw both my arms up to the sky – instead I turned a couple of somersaults. I spent 1,000 yen on colors and canvases and donated the rest to institutions for handicapped people. People said I was so poor I should have kept the money for myself but it just seemed too much for me.'

Iwao's gesture proved the parable of bread cast upon the waters. A newspaper ran the story of how a mouth-painting artist had given away most of the money he had earned from his first sale, and the story was picked up by the Association of Mouth and Foot Painting Artists who have first got to hear of many of their members through the press. Iwao was enrolled as a student and paid a monthly stipend which came just at the right moment as the company he worked for went bankrupt.

Two years later, in 1965, he was made a full member of the Association and his financial future was assured. Now he was able to paint as he has always wished to paint and he went from success to success with frequent exhibitions.

'There is a saying "The world is as kind as it is cruel",' says Iwao and then proceeds to tell the story of the unusual way he met his wife in 1969. In the autumn of that year he returned home from sketching Lake Biwa for a picture he wanted to enter in an exhibition. A newspaper reported how after the picture won a prize,

Iwao had presented it to an institution for the handicapped known as the Blue Sky Special School. As a result, he was inundated with letters from readers.

'It was hard work writing answers to all of them,' he says. 'For some unknown reason I left one unanswered. It was from a woman named Shoko Hidaka who worked in a beauty parlor. I felt very sorry that I had left her out so I found her telephone number and phoned her.

'"Is that Miss Hidaka?" I asked and she replied, "Ah, you are Mr. Adachi." I was surprised that she knew it was me when I phoned her for the first time but from then on we had telephone conversations and exchanged letters.

'One day she phoned me and said "Please take me somewhere this Monday."

'"How about Nara Park?" I suggested and as we had never met we described ourselves and arranged to meet on the platform of Truruhashi Station. Next Monday I learned her life story in the park and we had a long conversation until we came to the temple of the great statue of Buddha where we both offered prayers.

'The next evening Shoko rang me up and from the other end of the line came the words, "If you think it would be good for you, please make me your bride. I have just phoned my mother in Kyushu and she agrees. So please marry me."

'Later I learned what she had asked of the Buddha – "I should like to live with a disabled person so please make it come true. I know hardships might lie ahead for me but that's OK."

'The great Buddha statue responded beautifully. Maybe I was not disabled in my heart and Shoko became my wife.'

In January 1970, the couple was married and towards the end of the year gave birth to a baby girl they named Emiko – the daughter whom Iwao declared 'gives me the energy for tomorrow.'

Glenn Barnett

"At peace with myself."

'Break my neck!' Like his teenage friends, Glenn Barnett shouted their usual cry as he poised to dive from a jetty in the same way that actors joke 'break a leg' before going on stage. But this time Glenn's light-hearted words were a grim prophecy. He dove twelve feet into two feet of water that, being deceptively clear, looked much deeper. An instant later he lay drowning with a broken neck and almost severed spinal cord.

'I remember in some sort of way calling out to God,' he says when describing his accident. 'Those few moments were the most unusual I have ever spent. I knew I was going to drown yet I didn't panic. There was no fear, just a calmness as I inhaled salt water.

'Suddenly there was a lot of splashing and a boy called Graham Eastern dragged me to the shore. I tried to thank him but I doubt if he heard me. In fact I did not see him again for twenty-eight years when he returned to Port Lincoln on holiday with his wife. I took them out to dinner and was able to thank him properly. I have had a fantastic life and it would have been terrible to have lost it then.'

Glenn was born in 1947 in Port Lincoln, a typical fishing town in South Australia, and as a boy he played football and he became an athletics champion. Eager to earn his own living, he left school at fourteen to work in the spare parts department of a motor company.

The last day of November 1962 was particularly hot even for the Australian summer and after work he and a friend went swimming in the sea to cool down. After an hour it was time for them to go to their Friday night session of table tennis and rather than walk back to the shore on the jetty they decided to swim. Glenn dove in and in his own words 'pile-dived into the sand at the

bottom'. Luckily, someone on the shore knew what to do and packed sand around Glenn's neck to give it support until the ambulance arrived. The next morning he was flown 150 miles to the Royal Adelaide Hospital where he had a tracheotomy followed by an operation to graft a bone to support his broken neck.

Perhaps because at the age of fifteen it was considered he could not immediately take the knowledge that he would be paralyzed for life, no one at the hospital explained his condition to him and for several weeks he lay in bed expecting to recover. It was only a nurse's accidental remark that made him realize that he would never walk again and, as he said, 'it felt as though my guts fell out.'

'There was no counseling in those days so I thought about it by myself over the weekend and I began to think that there were still things I could do in a wheelchair. Then I was transferred to the Spinal Injuries Unit at the Morris Hospital where I saw my fellow quadriplegics with their hands crippled up, and I realized I had not only lost my legs but also my arms and I felt devastated.'

At the end on the year it was decided that nothing more could be done for Glenn and he was sent home to his parents – something that filled him with dismay. In the hospital he felt secure among people disabled like himself but he was terrified of being stared at in the world of the able bodied.

At first he refused to go outside the house, then he permitted himself to be wheeled on to the back veranda out of sight of the neighbors. It was his sister's sixteen-year-old boyfriend (now Glenn's brother-in-law) who altered this. He invited Glenn to a friend's house and, when Glenn as usual refused, he grabbed the wheelchair handles and raced down the drive with it and up the road with its occupant swearing at him in frustrated fury. As it turned out this action was one of the best experiences of Glenn's life as it broke down the barrier he was erecting against the outside world. After that he lived as normal a life as possible, going out to drive-in cinemas and parties.

One day a little boy who was being looked after by Glenn's mother asked him to draw him a picture. Glenn explained that he could not use his hands but the next day he thought he would try with a pen held in his mouth.

'I found it easy to draw lines fairly straight and I asked my mother to buy me some cheap watercolors and I began to splash about the paint,' he explains. 'It developed slowly and I enjoyed it. In fact I felt very pleased with the results and it was only later that I realized how terrible they were. In such a situation you are encouraged with false praise when you start painting.'

In 1966 Glenn's mother had another child and because of a difficult pregnancy was unable to continue looking after him so he returned to the Morris Hospital as a long-termer. Here he thought about life very deeply. His parents had been told he could expect to live for about twenty-five years. How would he fill them? It seemed impossible to have a relationship with a member of the opposite sex, impossible to work and impossible to take part in sport which had been the most important aspect of his life. The answer was provided by his fellow long term patients – pleasure! This group decided that all that was left in life was pleasure obtained largely through smuggled-in alcohol.

Then, at the age of twenty-two, something very significant happened in Glenn's life. A new gardener came to work in the hospital grounds. He was a Pentecostal Christian and he urged Glenn to read the New Testament. Having been taught as a boy to respect his elders Glenn complied and spent the next few months studying the Gospels.

'The result was that I felt challenged personally,' Glenn declared. 'A radical change came over me. My whole philosophy spun round and my need for pleasure was completely altered. I saw everything in a new way from then on, even things in nature, and I became a Christian.'

At that time Glenn had begun a deep friendship with one of the nurses at the hospital, Avril Saunders. As their relationship deepened they discussed the question of marriage but decided that it would be out of the question, not because of Glenn's disability but because it seemed impossible for them to live independently as man and wife.

Ever since his mother had bought him a box of watercolors Glenn had continued to paint even through his hangover days and, having seen a program on television on a mouth-painter, he got in touch with the Association of Mouth and Foot Painting Artists. He was so encouraged at the possibility of being able to make a living out of his art that he and Avril were married in 1971 in front of a congregation of 175 relations and friends. He was accepted as a full member by the Association two years later which meant that they were able to build a house in Adelaide Hills designed specially to suit a wheelchair.

Here Glenn settled down to a happy life with his wife and often painted up to eight hours a day.

'Now I felt challenged by God to learn as much as I could and I began correspondence courses with Bible colleges,' he recalls. 'In 1976 I was accepted into the South Australian Bible College where alterations were actually made to the building to accommodate my wheelchair.'

After three years Glenn received his Diploma of Divinity with distinction and was then offered a post as lecturer at the Uniting Church's Alcorn College, a lay training center. While involved in this work he also studied for a university degree.

He was given no special advantages, no extra time to sit examinations even though he had to write his papers with a pen held in his mouth. In one three-hour exam he filled eighteen pages this way.

Having gone so far in lay work, Glenn now felt inspired to go further. From 1981 to 1983 he studied at Trinity College, Brisbane, and was ordained as a Minister of the Uniting Church in 1984. His first parochial work was at Bundaberg in the heart of Queensland's cane and cattle country.

In an interview Glenn told a journalist, 'I loved parish ministry and the wheelchair presented no difficulties. I have been able to perform weddings and funerals, even in the mud at the graveside.'

His ministry was very much a team effort with Avril acting as his chauffeur, sounding board and critic.

Sadly for Glenn in 1989 he received a severe jolt in a car in which he was traveling which affected his neck so that, despite an operation, his condition deteriorated and it became necessary for him to give up church work in 1991. For his 'retirement' he and Avril bought a house in his home town of Port Lincoln, and here Glenn continued to paint as enthusiastically as ever, and even gained his Master of Arts degree in 1992.

'I find painting totally fulfilling,' he declares. 'I see it as something more than just pictures because I believe art stimulates peoples' thoughts about reality. I am often told that I must be at peace with myself because my work demonstrates peace, and I think that's true.

'I paint mainly landscapes, traveling all over Australia with Avril to get subjects and camping out in the heart of the bush.'

In talking to Glenn one finds that while his conversation may be serious it never strays far from humor. A discussion on philosophy might suddenly turn into an anecdote on how at his sister's wedding something went wrong with the portable plumbing required through his disability, with the result that as the wheelchair progressed down the church it left a trickle the length of the aisle, or how on his first day in a new parish the lifting device to help him out of the car broke and sent him sprawling full length at the feet of the minister he was to work with.

'I am one of those people who can never accept my disability,' he declares. 'To me it is silly to say I accept it – of course I would rather be able to walk! You adjust to rather than accept disability, and I have managed to do this through my artwork and as a Christian. Avril and I have had a happy and amazing life together and we could not have done this without me being able to earn my living as an artist.'

Eros Bonamini

"By chance I discovered painting."

Eros Bonamini was born in Verona, Italy, in 1942 and such is his affection for his hometown that he uses the pseudonym "Veronese" to sign his paintings. At school he studied technical subjects and had a love of mathematics, and it is doubtful if it ever crossed his mind that one day he would be a painter. But whatever plans he had for his future ended abruptly one day in 1960.

Although not a dedicated sportsman, he enjoyed games, swimming and diving and, as with a number of artists in the pages of this book, it was a diving accident that caused him to be paralyzed from the neck down. When he had recovered sufficiently from the ordeal he returned home where he was confined to a wheelchair.

'After the accident I often found myself alone and with a great deal of time to think,' he says. 'To pass the time I threw myself into literature and then by chance I discovered painting which opened up an entirely new vista for me. Since then I have dedicated myself entirely to painting.'

From the moment he first had the handle of a paint brush positioned between his teeth, Eros developed his latent talent at a remarkable rate. The director of a publishing house in Verona became interested when he heard of the young man who was painting by means of his mouth, and he visited Eros in his home. He was highly impressed by the work he saw and introduced it to the Association of Mouth and Foot Painting Artists. In March 1966 Eros joined the Association and was later voted on to the Board.

Although Eros began as a pictorial painter, his lively mind began considering the more abstract elements of art, especially Cubism. This artistic movement owed its origins to Picasso and Braque in 1907 and it rapidly influenced Western painting. In Cubism, the artist divided the subject of his picture into a number of parts and depicted differing aspects of it on the same canvas.

Eros explains, 'Cubism has interested me because it is an operation on time made up of the simultaneity of the artist's point of view so that an object and a landscape presented simultaneously on the same canvas shows a complex reality. And this was perhaps the start of my particular work on time – I should say, my curiosity on the operation of time.'

Perhaps it was his early study of mathematics that inspired Eros to explore the nature of time through the medium of art. But such an exploration could not be undertaken with conventional paint and canvas, the artist devised his own materials to undertake the quest which is charted in his book "Cronotopografie".

An idea of how Eros developed his materials and technique was given in an article by the critic Alberto Veca in which he explained that cement and adhesive were first treated as pigment.

'Then Bonamini enquired into the hardening process of the material, working on it with an incision of constant form and pressure,' he wrote. 'The outcome was a succession of scratches which tended to disappear as the drying process was completed. The variation of the adhesives signified a different behavior on the material: a matter of wishing to associate the constant differentiated reaction of the cement in the face of the same aggressive process.

'This was the reasoning on the "relativity" of the means and on the outcome which was accepted on its merits as a direct and true testimony of the working process. One must, together with this, look at a further enquiry made by Bonamini into materials in about 1977 when the scratch on the cement was replaced by ribbons of canvas soaked in different strengths of peroxide and, successively, placed in ink for a constant time. The result – each strip corresponds to a specific degree of absorption of the ink – becomes part of a sequence in which the various elements are displayed in succession, evidencing in its horizontal layout, the diversity of the physical results in the presence of the identity of the gestures.'

To those not familiar with the language of abstract art the above may certainly seem esoteric, but art depends on innovation if it is not to decline. The great artists of the 20th century all added to the progress of art by experimentation. And how successful has Eros Bonamini been in his development of new modes of expression related to his 'curiosity on the operation of time'?

In an introduction to Eros Bonamini's book "Cronotopografie" the art critic Eugenio Miccini declared, 'I have known very few artists of such clear intelligence and equally vivacious irony. For the past twenty years he has continued to develop constantly and coherently his research, by finding himself out of step with certain of today's artistic expressions.'

And the art expert Giorgio Cortenova has written, 'Following all his works over the years... I feel it fair to state that it is rare for an artist of our time to be able coherently to renew and enrich his work as does Bonamini. What is more, I cannot hide the intense feelings I have, the sensation his work gives me.'

It is not just the words of art critics that endorse his work but the large number of exhibitions around the world in which it has appeared. While he proclaims his ideas in abstract art he also paints still lifes and landscapes.

His work, that some call avant garde, is an example of how members of the MFPA develop their own styles. There are over six hundred such artists in the world and they have over six hundred approaches to art.

Eros Bonamini the artist is famous. Eros Bonamini the man is reserved when it comes to speaking about himself. To him it is his pictures that count and in "Cronotopografie", not a single mention is made of the fact that he is disabled.

To the author he did go so far as to say, 'I have all the interests of ordinary mortals – sometimes more important, sometimes less important. I love to travel a lot, I love many things... I am married and my wife is called Giuseppina – at home we call her "Giusi" – and my parents in their own house are not far from our home.

'I have no religious conviction though I have a religious culture, having been educated in a certain way but I am very logical – absolutely logical! – and to someone who has had my kind of experience in life I would say that culture is an option and can become a reason for living.'

In October 2002 Eros Bonamini was elected President of the Association worldwide.

Ruth Christensen

"It is as though something takes over."

One day when Ruth Christensen was eleven years old she was enjoying a bike ride with a friend when she approached a level crossing notorious for its poor visibility. She pedaled on to it, had a fleeting impression of a locomotive looming above her... then nothing. She has no recollection of the actual accident which she still finds difficult to discuss, only coming around in a hospital bed to discover that both her arms had been severed above the elbow. It was the beginning of her long fight to regain the normal expectations of life that seemed to have ended at the level crossing.

Today Ruth says, 'It was a hard struggle but one gains strength from having to struggle like I did.'

One of a very happy family of five children, Ruth was born in 1929 at Lynge in Nordsjalland, Denmark.

'You can imagine how my accident cast a shadow over our lives that up until then had been so carefree. That was one of the reasons why, when I came out of hospital, I was determined to get back to as normal a life as possible. I really struggled to manage with everyday things, and gradually I began to succeed.

'I used my mouth to put on my doll's clothes, turn the pages of my book and I tried to write holding a pen in my teeth which was far from easy. The good thing was that I was able to keep going to my usual school. My father made an appliance which, attached to what remained of my upper arms, enabled me to use a fork so that I was no longer dependent on someone feeding me.'

It had been Ruth's childhood dream to become an artist, an ambition that remained despite the accident, and after she completed her school course she applied to be enrolled in an art school in Copenhagen but was bitterly disappointed by the response she received. She was told it would be far too difficult for someone without hands. In reply Ruth demonstrated her ability to draw with mouth-held pencils – and was accepted. She commuted by train to Copenhagen for her lessons until the family moved to the capital, buying a house in the Vanlise suburb where Ruth lives today.

After art college, Ruth's standard of work was good enough to get her work in various advertising agencies.

'I did all sorts of work-brochures, catalogs and advertisements, and I created designs for a linen manufacturer. It seemed that I had got over my handicap in that I was living a more active life than most. In 1960 I went to Canada to work in an advertising agency in Montreal.'

Ruth recalls this period as one of the most exciting. She learned a lot, was surrounded by friends with whom she traveled to the USA and fell in love with the man she hoped to marry. The wedding took place in Copenhagen in 1964.

Ruth and her husband settled in Nordsjalland where to Ruth's huge delight, her son Thomas was born. She continued to freelance as an advertising artist which was to be of benefit when the marriage ended after nine years. Ruth returned to Copenhagen with Thomas where she moved into the upper story of her parents' house where she had a studio for her freelance work, but she found it a struggle financially.

The break-through in her career came when the MFK – the Danish branch of the Mouth and Foot Painting Artists' Association – heard about her work and offered her a scholarship. In 1982 she became a full member of the MFPA.

'To become a member of such a partnership and receive a regular income was a marvelous lifting of my problems. It has made it possible for me to develop my own painting, as it was always my ambition to do. Working in my own way gives me freedom. In the beginning when it came to painting I wanted to do everything correctly – to paint everything exactly the way it looked, but as I learned more I dared to go my own way.

'I get ideas from actual things and like to go around with my sketch pad, and when I get back to my studio I look at my sketches and let my imagination have full rein. When I decide what to do I make a drawing on the canvas, begin to apply the color and then the painting goes its own way. It is as though something takes over.'

It seems to Ruth that her work develops a life of its own in the way that some writers believe their characters form their own independent personalities.

'Although I like to work with watercolors best I find that by switching to different mediums and trying new techniques I do not get stale. For this reason I try to use oil paints sometimes but I find the pigment heavy. When I do use oils I do so as if they are watercolors, applying them in thin transparent layers which are easy to work over.'

One motif that has long fascinated Ruth is that of a glass flower in a vase with light streaming through it and a view of a room behind distorted by light refraction. It is one of the hardest subjects for an artist to tackle but she has returned to it many times.

The many greetings cards that Ruth has painted are not only known in Scandinavia but are published internationally. She believes that a key to their success is the fact that she has worked as an advertising artist – the message of her cards is direct and people respond to it immediately.

Looking back on her life Ruth admits that she has 'had it good'.

'Life is easier for me than most other members of the Association in that I can walk freely,' she says. 'I am able to use a car with the help of special steering equipment and in summer I spend time in a house on the coast which charges my batteries. I am also very lucky that I am on close terms with my family. Best of all is the fact that I have the opportunity to paint without economic pressure. It is painting that I want to continue with for as long as I am capable of working.'

In 1992 the Council of Europe announced that its official Christmas card for that year would be designed by a mouth or foot painter. When the final painting was chosen from the large number that had been submitted it was Ruth Christensen's 'Christmas in Europe' which depicted a snow scene with merry children in Santa Claus costumes pulling a sleigh loaded with lettered building blocks spelling out 'Europa-Europe'. As a result hundreds of thousands of people around the world became aware that 'art without hands' is not only possible but can be highly professional.

This aspect of the competition delighted Ruth, as she is an enthusiastic worker on behalf of her fellow disabled artists, especially those in Scandinavia whom she represents after being elected an AMFPA Board member. Not only does she travel to the Association's headquarters in Vaduz twice a year to confer with other Board members in the Association's 'Parliament' but, in company with her sister Lis, she tours the Nordic countries visiting artists to discuss their ideas and well-being.

Kun-Shan Hsieh

"Suddenly I entered a world of my own."

'I owe so much to the loving care of my mother.' These words have been repeated over and over by Kun-Shan Hsieh when giving interviews to journalists about his art and life. Yet no matter how many times this phrase has been quoted it never loses its sincerity as far as Kun-Shan is concerned. He can never forget that after his accident a number of his relatives and family friends were full of suggestions as to how his parents could rid themselves of the liability of a severely disabled son. His mother's reply was to insist on being with him no matter what the future held.

Inspired by her love and devotion, Kun-Shan was determined to defy all the odds against him and not let her down.

He was born in Taitung in eastern Taiwan in 1958. His parents were poor peasants but their economic situation – five family members sharing one small apartment – in no way prevented the boy from enjoying a happy childhood. In due course he attended an elementary school and when he completed his basic education he regarded himself as lucky when he found work in a garment factory.

In 1972 word spread among the staff that they were going to be relocated in a new factory and Kun-Shan was excited, and enthusiastically joined in the work of removing machinery from the old plant. It was a break in the rather dull routine of factory life and the youth was in high spirits as he helped load a truck. Grasping a piece of metal he lifted it high to place it on top of the pile forgetting how high he was above the ground.

The metal touched a high voltage cable overhead and a devastating burst of electricity surged through it and the youth who was holding it. Kun-Shan was rushed to hospital, where in order to save his life doctors carried out drastic surgery. When he finally recovered consciousness, it was to find that his entire left arm had been amputated, as had three-quarters of his right arm and his right leg at the knee. No wonder friends of the Hsieh family shook their heads – a youth with only one limb left would be a terrible burden on those who were already hard pressed in the struggle for existence. There must be a way in which this responsibility could be shed...

And it was at this point that Kun-Shan's mother declared her devotion to her disabled son, which at that time, was the only ray of light in his darkened world. In those days there was no sophisticated equipment or training programs to help someone so handicapped, no computers that could be worked with a mouthstick or electric wheelchairs that could be controlled electronically through the movement of the patient's chin.

Months passed as Kun-Shan slowly recovered from the surgery he had undergone, and he continually asked himself what the future could hold for someone who had lost the use of their body. And as the months became years the question remained unanswered.

It was in 1980 that this maimed garment-worker discovered the creative pleasure of painting. Up until then he had passed the time by endeavoring to draw simple sketches with a pencil held between his teeth, then one day he tried 'doodling' with a paintbrush.

'Suddenly I entered a world of my own,' he explains. 'All the loneliness, frustration and pain disappeared when I was painting.'

There is a long way to go between doodling and producing an actual painting, but having discovered his new world, Kun-Shan was determined to make the journey. At the beginning, he practiced for ten hours to get the necessary control. Sometimes he was so exhausted that he would fall asleep in front of his picture.

'Painting was so much on my mind that sometimes I would wake up with a start and immediately begin to add a few strokes on an unfinished canvas,' he says.

When he felt confident that he could control the brush in this way he attended art classes to learn the essentials of what was to be his unexpected profession. As his technique improved word began to spread about this young artist and in 1985, when he held his first one-man exhibition in Taipei, the leading Taiwan artist Shiuan-shan Wu told the Press, 'He is fast becoming one of the best in his generation. There is a special touch of humanity in his paintings.'

Reuter's correspondent covered the exhibition for the media outside Taiwan with the result that an article about Kun-Shan appeared in the Reader's Digest.

'In a country still primarily interested in Chinese watercolors and calligraphy, Hsieh's paintings have created a new interest in oils,' the Digest declared. It also quoted Chau-chu Ho, a committee member of the Taiwan Oil Painting Association, who in speaking of Kun-Shan, stated, 'He has set an example to all the handicapped that they are not a burden on society but rather a creative force if they are given the opportunity.'

The Taipei exhibition was a great success not only because all thirty-two of the paintings exhibited found buyers but also because the Press report led to the Association of Mouth and Foot Painting Artists contacting Kun-Shan through the gallery where his exhibition had been held. The same year he was invited to join the organization.

Since then Kun-Shan's reputation has continued to grow. What is intriguing about his work is the fact that he is at ease with both European and traditional Chinese techniques. His favorite motifs are flowers and animals and an example of his typical traditional work shows a pair of birds with bright plumage amid the most delicately tinted blooms. Another picture with a European influence depicts flowers in blue flowerpots painted with bold impressionistic strokes in gaudy colors that seem to radiate sunshine and heat. It seems remarkable that two such differing paintings could be the work of the same artist.

In speaking about his work he declares that he still wants to learn more about painting and that it is his aim to establish a unique style of his own that will reflect in his works.

Apart from giving Kun-Shan a profession, his involvement in art led indirectly to the happiest aspect of his life. In 1980, when his interest in painting had begun to change his life, he visited a friend at his studio near Taipei. Here he met a charming girl named Su-Fen Line and was greatly attracted to her. In 1987 they were married and today they have two daughters, Ning who was born in 1989 and Hsuen who was born in 1992. One of Kun-Shan's chief delights is to go swimming with his daughters.

Apart from painting and his family, his greatest enjoyment is in travel and his other interests include Chinese Chess, watching ball games and singing – a full life for one who once it seemed had nothing to look forward to.

Soon-Yi Oh

"I learned with a mixture of anguish and patience."

The river that flowed past the home of little Soon-Yi Oh in MaSan, South Korea, was cool and inviting on a hot summer's day in 1968. In company with half a dozen children, all four or five years older than herself, three-year-old Soon-Yi toddled to the river's edge to bathe and get cool. She knew that her older companions would see that she came to no harm in the water and added to her sense of security was the fact that she could see her parents' house on the other side of the railway line that ran beside the river bank.

For a while the children played at the water's edge, laughing and splashing until they decided it was time to leave the river. Laughing, they raced up the bank with Soon-Yi following them. They had just reached the railway track when a locomotive came into view.

Like Ruth Christensen – who had a similar accident – Soon-Yi has no recollection of what happened next, of how the older children scattered to safety. Not nimble enough to get clear, she was struck by the on-coming engine and both her arms were amputated. What she does remember is that the following years were very miserable ones.

Born in 1966 Soon-Yi had two brothers and two sisters in what she describes as an 'ordinary family', her father being a carpenter. Looking back on her early days she says, 'There were many people who have had an influence on me, those among my family, teachers and friends who were concerned about my education, especially the fine arts.'

Despite the pain and frustration she suffered after her accident, by the age of five she was able to use her foot for everyday tasks with almost the same dexterity that able-bodied children use their hands. She attended primary school and it was in her fourth year there that her teacher suggested that she should try painting with a brush held between her toes. The effect that this had on the ten-year-old was profound.

'I am sure I was destined to work in an artistic field whether I was to be handicapped or not,' she says. 'I have painted every day since the age of ten.' Yet the fact that she felt she had found her metier through brush and canvas did not mean that foot painting came to her easily.

'I learned painting with difficulty,' she recalls. 'I learned with a mixture of anguish and patience. Although it was a time of suffering, once I started learning to paint I could not get the thought of art out of my mind. One practical advantage I had was that, because I had used my foot as a hand from an early age, I had the strength to use a brush. And when I found I could perform an exact function such as drawing a line I was tremendously encouraged. But I still have difficulty in expressing the more elaborate parts of my pictures but with effort I shall achieve greater skill.'

Soon-Yi is a perfectionist. In looking at her delicate and evocative landscapes it is hard to imagine that she has difficulty with the 'more elaborate parts'.

In 1985 when she was nineteen her painstaking efforts were rewarded by winning first prize in the National High School Students' Art Contest which was sponsored by Hongik University. Television cameras presented the awards ceremony to South Korea and the carpenter's daughter who, sixteen years earlier had fallen under a train, had her first taste of fame.

The prize was not only a recognition that Soon-Yi's mouth-held brush could produce pictures that were judged ahead of those by her able-bodied fellows, but the publicity it generated led her to being invited to become a student of the Association of Mouth and Foot Painting Artists. This support was to prove of immense help to her when she enrolled at Dun Kug University to study Fine Arts.

'When I entered as a freshman I found many unexpected difficulties,' she said. 'But I received financial help from the Association. After graduating in 1990 I continued my studies in Taipei and then went to the graduate school of the National Academy of Fine Arts in the People's Republic of China. Here I studied the history of art, art criticism and, of course, painting.'

Speaking of her work Soon-Yi explains, 'I think a great deal and meditate before I start painting. It takes a long time for me to finish a painting and therefore I always study the challenges that it is going to present. The motifs I like to work on are from nature – landscapes and studies of four plants that I find particularly graceful – plum, orchid, chrysanthemums and bamboo – and sometimes I like to work these into abstract paintings.

'I have a great feeling of achievement when I finish a work, though in my opinion the process of reaching the goal is more important. Above all what I strive for is to be faithful to myself. It is my dream to accomplish work of the finest quality.

'I had a hard time learning art but I think I have overcome the difficulties through the expression of my mind into paintings. I had to deal with blue moods and disappointments which I overcame by devoting myself to meditating, reading and above all painting.

'I have always wanted to become an example to other handicapped people. To those who find themselves in circumstances like mine, I would say that they should strive to do their best at all times with a clear mind and cultivate understanding for other people.'

Jayantilal Shihora

"I have taken many steps forward."

'Without his hands there will be nothing that Jayantilal will be able to do.' When Jayantilal Shihora overheard these words spoken by a relative they filled him with pain more intense than the physical pain that he had suffered during the previous months. That pain had begun on the night of Diwali, the Hindu Festival of Lights. Fourteen-year-old Shihora was ducking excitedly through the crowds that filled the town of Bhavnagar in the Indian state of Gujarat. Houses were illuminated with traditional oil lamps and everywhere there was the report of crackers and lurid explosions of color from fireworks while in the temples, ceremonies were held in honor of the goddesses Lakshmi and Kali.

Suddenly Jayantilal's laughter turned to a scream as his arms were engulfed in a gush of firework flame and his life was changed forever.

He had been born a normal healthy child, the son of a grain merchant.

'My father was very kind but in my early childhood I was deprived of maternal love when my mother died,' he says. 'My father married again and within three months of that my elder brother died of brain fever. After this shock my sister married so that I was left very lonely.'

During this unhappy period Jayantilal sought comfort by dreaming about his future. He would become an engineer – a teacher – perhaps a doctor – at least a man with a good profession. Such dreams ended with the explosion of a firework at Diwali and the necessity of him having his hands amputated.

The months that followed he describes as a 'dark period of depression', and when the pain of his injuries began to fade it was replaced by the remark of his relative which brought home to him the hopelessness of his future. His previous ambitions mocked him and he could not stop asking himself, 'Am I a useless person?'

It was then that Jayantilal underwent what might be described as a mystical experience. In answer to his nightly question about himself it seemed that he heard an inner voice. Describing it to the author he said, 'I heard words that seemed to come from some great teacher – "You have lost only your hands but not your mind or soul." After that I felt my confidence awaken.'

From that moment on the boy endeavored to do things for himself. Many times his efforts were met with failure but when he succeeded in performing some normally simple action it was one more step on the long road to rehabilitation. Somehow he learned to eat with a spoon despite the fact that his arms ended just below the elbows, and his greatest triumph came when he managed to ride a bicycle 'no hands'. As time passed be became far less dependent on others, but he was still faced with the question of how to earn a living.

Five years after the Diwali misfortune, a friend named Giriraj Bhartiya sent Jayantilal some postcards from Calcutta.

These greetings cards were a revelation because their scenes had been painted by disabled artists using brushes either held in their mouth or between their toes.

'Why can't I do this?' Jayantilal asked himself. From then on he spent hours at a time with a pen clamped between his teeth endeavoring to write. At first he experienced the frustrations encountered by most disabled people when they begin the often painful task of learning to control a pen or pencil whose point is only inches away from their eyes. Things would go well and then the work would be ruined as the pen faltered and slid across the page or the ache of fatigue led to disheartening results.

But, still inspired by his 'voice' and the success of the handicapped painters, he persevered. Finally he began to manipulate a paintbrush as well as a pen. Using either oils or watercolors, he painted landscapes and in 1963 decided it was time to get in touch with the organization that had produced the cards which had inspired him. As a result he was awarded a scholarship by the Association of Mouth and Foot Painting Artists.

'At that time I was the only Indian member,' he recalls. 'I was so happy I worked harder than ever, and I remembered the saying "When God closes one door, He opens a second."'

Now that he received a regular stipend Jayantilal was able to study in the Faculty of Fine Arts at Baroda University. In 1964 he won first prize for art from the Lalit Kala Academy in Gujarat and from then on success followed success. Soon afterwards he received a prize for his work from the Kenny Rehabilitation Institute of Chicago and his first one-man exhibition was held in Bombay. Since then there have been many more awards and exhibitions.

The Press took up his story and a sentence in The Indian Express was typical of the journalists' reaction to him – 'The painter from Bhavnagar has no hands but plenty of spirit.'

Inspired equally by European classical painters and traditional Indian art, Jayantilal has developed his distinctive style.

'In the beginning I painted landscapes and sea scenes,' he says, 'but later I concentrated on folk art using tempera colors. I love nature and like to ramble by the seashore, in woods and on the hills and from this I seem to get strength and inspiration for my creative work. I like lonely places where I feel that the natural things about me are my friends. In particular I like to sit in silence on the shore of a lake at sunset which is a very special time for me.'

The year 1974 was an exciting one for Jayantilal. In it he married Kiran Mahta, a Bachelor of Arts, who, luckily for her husband, shares his passion for nature and wandering off the beaten track.

'This was a love marriage,' he says emphatically. 'And thanks to the support Kiran gave me I have taken many steps forward with my painting. And we have two sons.'

As the Festival of Diwali comes around in October or November each year Jayantilal, now an associate member of the MFPA, cannot help being reminded of the accident that robbed him of his hands but none of the despair that once haunted him remains. He has found his profession and as he once told a reporter, 'I do by my mouth what other artists do by their hands – there is no other difference.'

Cristobal Toledo

"All of life is beautiful."

Cristobal Moreno-Toledo came into the world on June 21, 1941 in the Castro del Rio in the province of Cordoba, Spain. Castro del Rio is renowned for its beauty and the fact that the author Miguel de Cervantes used it as a background for his novel Don Quixote – according to local legend he was imprisoned in the town when, as a collector of taxes, he fell foul of the Church. It is understandable that Cristobal has always loved his home town, the ambience that inspired Don Quixote to set forth to challenge the world also inspired him to tilt at the windmills of despair that cast shadows over the disabled.

Until the age of four Cristobal was like any other lively little boy but then his parents became aware of disquieting symptoms and progressive muscular dystrophy was diagnosed – the relatively rare disease usually begins in childhood and continues to waste the muscles for up to twenty years, leaving the affected areas without power of movement.

Doctors decided that the condition could be relieved by surgery. Each time the child was admitted to hospital there was an upsurge of hope, only to be dashed when it became clear that the operation had not been a success and as his legs became affected it became necessary for him to use a wheelchair. Before the encroaching disease deprived Cristobal of the use of his arms he was often seen racing in his wheelchair through the town's maze of winding streets in a way that could only be described as stylish. And style is something that he has retained down the years despite his disability.

Because of his weak condition, which followed each operation, he was forced to spend lonely hours at home with the result that, while his friends played football, he retired into the world of his imagination and, to quote the writer

Francisco Zueras, 'he used his time to develop his profound intellect.'

When Cristobal reached the age of thirteen he had lost the use of his hands but this did not stop him from falling wildly in love with a school mistress and, eager to appreciate the things that were of importance to her, he developed a keen interest in literature. He found it to be something that had the power to take him away from the world of the wheelchair on wonderful flights of fancy. The books he read inspired him with the idea of becoming an author and he realized that the first requirement of a writer is to be able to physically write.

To this end he experimented with holding a pencil between his teeth and before long he mastered the technique. It then occurred to him that if he could write this way he could also draw and his artistic career began. He entered into this new pursuit with his usual enthusiasm, teaching himself to paint everyday objects and scenes of the gentle landscape that surrounds his town. Later he took a correspondence course in artwork and, when he felt confident in the techniques of painting, he developed a distinctive style by generously applying colors with a mouth-held spatula.

It was while he was training himself to become an artist that Cristobal struck up a friendship with a young man named Javier Criado who was to trigger a turning point in his life. The two shared many interests and one day in 1962 Javier excitedly told him about a journal known as Artis-Muti, the official publication of an organization devoted to the promotion of severely disabled artists known as the Association of Mouth and Foot Painting Artists.

Prompted by his friend, Cristobal sent some of his drawings to the Associations in Madrid where they were immediately dispatched to the head office in Vaduz, Liechtenstein, to be placed in an exhibition. In March he was awarded a scholarship and then to his amazement and delight he received the news that he had been made a life member of the Association. This meant that from now on he could concentrate on art without any financial worries.

As his paintings appeared in more exhibitions his work began to show Impressionist influences and from that time he has demonstrated his versatility as an artist. To look through a catalog of his work one sees powerful studies of people – a beggar woman with her child, a reclining nude, a farmer riding his donkey, a late night procession – all come to life on his canvases. Then there are still life studies of fruit, fish laid out ready for the pot, and portraits which have a delicacy associated with crayons that are in contrast to his bold spatula-applied oils.

Turning from canvas and paper he created a series of mother-and-child studies on ceramic tiles, and he has also ventured into the field of modernistic sculpture, designing fantastic figures out of pieces of metal welded together. As it is impossible for him to do such work with his useless hands he sits in his wheelchair while a technician cuts the metal to his directions.

In 1993 Cristobal went to Rome where Pope John Paul II granted an audience to MFPA members in St. Peter's Church. During the audience he presented the late Pope with a large portrait he had painted of him. In return he was given a Papal plaque as a mark of esteem and Marlyse Tovae, then President of the Association, received a letter from a Vatican official, part of which read, '...may I kindly inform you that His Holiness has instructed me to convey to you sincere thanks... for the presentation of the painting by the Spanish artist Cristobal Moreno-Toledo. From his heart the Holy Father prays to God to protect and assist you, the esteemed members of the AMFPA and all those close to them.'

Cristobal has received many distinctions in his own country, France and the USA. To be working at something one loves and to receive recognition for it is a great achievement for a man with no use in his limbs. Yet it is not enough for this quietly spoken artist with the flowing hair and a goatee beard. There is also his art gallery.

In Castro del Rio stands a picturesque gateway with a tiled arch, wrought ironwork and a guardian statue of a figure on classical drapery. Beyond this is the gallery which Cristobal set up for the purpose of exhibiting the work of little known artists.

This artist has come a long way since as a lonely boy he first put a pencil between his teeth, but the spark of his creativity is as bright as ever. He is a man who obviously loves life and he sums up his credo with the words, 'All of life is beautiful.'

Iwao Adachi Mount Fuji

Iwao Adachi
Osaka-Jo Castle

Iwao Adachi   Castle Neuschwanstein, Bavaria

Iwao Adachi   Rothenburg, Romantic Street

Glenn Barnett Winter Landscape

Glenn Barnett Coastal Landscape

Glenn Barnett   Red Rock

Glenn Barnett   By the Lake

Eros Bonamini
Canal in Venice

Eros Bonamini
Still Life

Eros Bonamini In the Studio

Overleaf:
Eros Bonamini
Porto Venere Harbor, Italy

Ruth Christensen Loving Animals

Kun-Shan Hsieh
Sunflowers in Vase

Kun-Shan Hsieh Fishes

Overleaf:
Kun-Shan Hsieh
Still Life, Flowers in Vases

Kun-Shan Hsieh Exotic Flowers

Kun-Shan Hsieh Birds by the Lake

Soon-Yi Oh
Birds on Tree

Soon-Yi Oh   Orchids in Vase

Soon-Yi Oh
White Magnolias

Soon-Yi Oh   Flowers

Jayantilal Shihora
Elephant Ride

Jayantilal Shihora   Fetching Water

Jayantilal Shihora   Guardian of the Oxen

Jayantilal Shihora   Working in the Field

José Uribe

"A whole new direction to my life."

From the very beginning my family felt I would never be able to lead an adequate life,' says José Uribe who, born in Dolores Hidalgo in central Mexico in 1963, came into the world without arms. 'They did not believe I would ever be able to walk, eat or move independently. They probably felt that I would always be a burden. My parents and brothers always had to carry me down the street and I always found it difficult to keep my balance because of the disproportionate length of my legs compared to the rest of my body. Inside the house I used to drag myself around on my bottom using my feet to propel me along.'

What must have affected the confidence of the child was the fact that he had three lively brothers and four equally lively sisters, and from an early stage the contrast between him and his active siblings was painfully apparent.

It seemed that everyone's mind was made up that José's case was hopeless. No one thought of trying to improve it until he was four years old when his grandmother held him upright and tried to get him to take a step in the way that one would encourage a baby.

After a while he did learn to take some stumbling steps and his uncle Luis bought him a baby-walker. At last he experienced the wonderful sensation of being able to move about the house on his own.

Two years later he no longer needed this help, he could walk by himself though he frequently fell over as his balance remained uncertain.

Just as it had been believed that José was incapable of walking, so it had been thought that it would be impossible for him to write or attend school. But after he had proved that he was capable of making progress his father put a pencil between the toes of his left foot and began teaching him to draw and form letters.

'My mother thought it would be a good idea for me to learn to read as at least it would give me something to occupy myself with – after all, I was never going to be able to go out to work,' he recalls. 'On my first day at school my teacher did not want to accept me into his class as he was afraid the children would give me a hard time. The headmaster finally persuaded him to take me in – and I found my classmates treated me with respect and were always asking me questions about my situation.'

While José was happy to attend his class he found the break an unhappy time. With nobody to look after him he was unable to go out to play and had to watch his friends having fun from a distance.

José's mischievous brother Juan Manuel also attended the school but was two years ahead of José. Each morning he would wheel him to school in a little cart and as he approached the gates he broke into a run so that he charged through them at a daredevil speed to the admiration of the pupils who waited for the display every morning – and to the terror of José.

In 1975 when José completed primary school, where he had become proficient at reading and foot-writing, he spent two years at the Institute of Rehabilitation in Mexico City. Here it was believed that his life could be improved by the fitting of mechanical arms, a project that was funded by the wife of the Governor of Guanajuato.

At first the boy was terrified that they would be grafted on to him by surgery thus making him part robot and he experienced a flood of relief when he was told that such drastic treatment was not necessary. Although he 'wore' his artificial limbs while he was at the Institute they were not a success. He had become so adept at using his feet that he found little benefit from them while on the other hand they were awkward, heavy and encroached on his sense of personal space. After his period at the Institute he gave up using them – thankfully.

While José had been at the center his ability at drawing was recognized and it had been hoped that his mechanical hands would further his skill. Unfortunately they lacked the necessary flexibility and he continued using his foot, copying sketches in order to master the technique of watercolor painting.

'In the second year at the Institute I became increasingly mindful of my physical state because I could observe other people in similar situations to mine,' he says. 'I also began to think very deeply about philosophical matters – fate, the purpose of existence, the boundaries of being, the infinite...'

These thoughts awakened such an interest in philosophy that José was determined to read the subject at the University of Guanajuato after completing his studies at preparatory college. It meant that he would have to leave his family and the support they provided, but to José the need to learn more was paramount.

'Living in the city of Guanajuato was an incredible experience,' he says. 'I got to know a lot a friends and people who would prove very supportive. I grew further and further apart from my family and became completely immersed in my new environment. Guanajuato is very much a cultural center and my university experience (I was enrolled at the School of Philosophy) gave me a new way of looking at things and my expectations began to change. There were so many opportunities to learn all sorts of subjects in this cultural hotbed and I took classes with the teacher Jorge Rocha who instilled in me the principles of still life.'

For his thesis José wrote "The Compositional Elements of Art" in which he set out the fundamentals of aesthetic analysis of paintings which had developed from his own practical work. Now this interest in painting took over his life and after he completed his philosophical studies he took a course at the School of Creative Studies under the direction of Patricia Van Vloten. Here he learned the techniques of oil painting and color blending and encaustic art, an ancient classical method of painting with colored waxes and 'fixing' them by heat.

By now José was beginning to receive recognition for his efforts. In 1987 the President of Mexico, Miguel de La Madrid, presented him with the First National Youth Award in the Presidential residence in Mexico City, and later he was to receive an accolade from a completely different quarter.

At the beginning of the eighties he had learned of the Association of Mouth and Foot Painting Artists from the well known Mexican foot painter Demetrio Herrera Olivares but he decided to work at his art until he felt it was of a satisfactory standard before approaching the organization. Then, in 1990, a selection of his work was parceled up and sent to the Association's headquarters in Liechtenstein.

'I was accepted for a scholarship by the Association, which meant I could concentrate on my creative output. If it had not been for the financial backing afforded by the Association, I would have found it very difficult to continue my chosen occupation, and I have been able to take courses in several different cities including Madrid, where I spent many months thanks again to the support of the Association.

'In March 1994 I became a full member of the Association. This gave me a whole new direction to my life both artistically and personally, and for this I am profoundly grateful.'

Speaking about his art José says, 'Some of my work has been influenced by religious images and constructions. City churches are remarkable edifices. I also work with still life and one of my favorite themes involves those objects associated with eating and drinking – bottles, bread and fruit. I also like to combine different objects such as a violin, a vase and a swatch of cloth.

JOSÉ URIBE

'Landscapes also fascinate me, mountains especially. Flat lands leave me cold as do the new towns that have wiped out the old urban landscape. However, the human figure is the greatest inspirer with all its postures, proportions and textures.'

An unusual aspect about José as a foot painter is that he uses his mouth as well, mainly to fill in backgrounds because that way he can cover a large area more quickly. But the detailed work is always done with a brush held in his toes as the foot allows him more flexibility.

'Physical disability can be a strong impediment and it is possible to fall into the trap of trying to shield oneself from the world,' José told the author. 'To avoid this feeling of limitation it is essential to maintain contact with friends and to take on a larger view of the world. The thing I value above all else is the companionship of friends. It is so important to spend time with those you love and to be able to share your worries and the things that make you happy. Love is central to everything and it is love that inspires the colors and forms I use in my art.'

Today José lives in the city of his birth, Dolores Hidalgo. He resides in his family's home where he has a well-lit studio separate from the house.

Trevor Wells

"I was amazed – I was actually painting."

As far as I was concerned the art period at school was a lesson in which you did as little as possible,' says Trevor Wells, one of the best known English mouth painting artists. 'All I was really interested in was sports. I was mad about it. Strangely enough, I still am though now I can only watch.'

On leaving school Trevor, who had been born in Portsmouth in 1956, became an apprentice carpenter and started playing rugby football for the Uxbridge Rugby Club on the outskirts of London. The highlight of his week came when he played with the rugby club in Uxbridge. The exhilaration of the game and the camaraderie that is traditionally associated with rugby players became one of the chief factors – if not the chief factor – in the young man's life.

One Sunday in September, 1978, Trevor's team set out for the grounds of the Twickenham Rugby Club where a 'beer match' – i.e. a Sunday game – had been arranged. Perhaps because it was a fun match Trevor did not take it as seriously as he should have.

'It was a terribly hot Indian summer,' he said. 'We were not keyed up before the game as usually happens. Normally you never put your boots on when you are on the field but this time we did which shows our relaxed mood. Once the game started there was a scrum. I must have been slow that day because I was too late getting my head down in the scrum. I was trapped and took the weight of the scrum on the back of my neck.'

Trevor was rushed by ambulance to London's Middlesex Hospital where it was found that his neck was broken at the C4 level. That evening he was transferred to Charing Cross Hospital for a spinal fusion and later taken to Stoke Mandeville Hospital which is world famous for the treatment of such cases. Here he remained

for six months and mentally came to terms with the fact that in those few seconds on the rugby pitch his life had completely changed. It was a difficult time for a 21-year-old who had lived for sport.

'I must confess I did a lot of heavy thinking there,' he said, 'but I like to think that I did not find it too difficult to accept the fact that I was now totally disabled. Of course it is hard to say so yourself, but I realized that I must not have the attitude of some who felt that the whole world was against them because of an accident. I knew I had to carry on but, as I said, there were times for some pretty deep thought.

'Having to cope with a quadriplegic would have been too big a burden for my mother so in April, 1979 I was transferred to the Alderbourne Unit at a hospital on the outskirts of London. It had only recently been opened and was designed to cater for long-term patients like me.' Because Trevor had managed to come to terms with the way his life had altered he found little trouble in adapting to life in the unit. One thing was certain, he harbored no resentment against the game that had been the cause of his misfortune. His enthusiasm for rugby remained undimmed and he watched it avidly on television and read the sports section in the newspapers, and in order to turn the pages he learned to use a mouthstick. In this way the days passed without Trevor doing anything except to follow his favorite sport on television. At times the thought that he was leading an empty existence troubled him but, he asked himself, what could he do to alter his life? There seemed to be no answer.

'Then someone suggested that I should have a go at painting,' he said. 'It was something I had never considered. I had no interest in art and painting was the last thing at which I thought I would be any good. On the other hand it would help to pass the time and I agreed to try. A paintbrush was fitted to my mouthstick, paints were laid out in front of me and I began. I must admit the result was pretty iffy, but when I was on my third picture I was amazed – I was actually painting!'

One reason he found little difficulty in using a paint brush was because he had his mouthstick attached to a rugby gum shield to distribute the weight evenly in his mouth. Thus no undue stress is placed upon the teeth as can be the case if they are clamped on a pencil or brush handle for long periods. As for the mouthstick itself, Trevor had an extremely light arrow shaft fitted to the gum shield and this device proved so effective that his writing is far neater today than when he was able to do it by hand.

It is typical of Trevor that when he talks about painting methods he makes it sound as though there is nothing to it.

'There are so few rules,' he says breezily. 'You just have to remember that you start with the background and work forward, that light against dark throws up color and so on.'

It sounds glib, but the truth is that Trevor had to strive hard to learn his craft. He never had any training and taught himself by trial and error. The possibility of becoming a professional painter was very far from Trevor's mind, it was his love of painting that continually urged him to improve his technique.

Discussing his work Trevor said, 'I do like snow and with the light it reflects you can get some lovely effects. Winter transforms everything and to me there is something magical about snowdrifts with the foot marks of animals printed on them, even the tire marks on a snow covered road.'

It can take up to four months for Trevor to complete a painting which seems a long time even for a mouth-painter but his pictures are built up with almost microscopic detail. He jokes that in order to get this effect some of his brushes have only two hairs.

Looking at his landscapes one gets the impression that every leaf on every tree is individually painted. This gives the effect of great clarity and reflects Trevor's dictum: 'I like to do scenes that you could walk into.'

By chance, relatives of a fellow patient in the unit happened to see some of Trevor's work. They were particularly interested because they knew the foot painting artist named Paul Driver who was a member of the MFPA. They suggested that Trevor should get in touch with the Association and, although he had never heard of the organization, he took the advice and submitted his work. As a result he became a student and two-and-a-half years later he was made a full member.

'I certainly could not survive on my own but through its marketing the Association makes it possible for me to earn a living with my paint brush,' Trevor explains. 'And I am lucky in that the scenes I like painting are commercial. It takes me a long time to complete a picture so I can see no point in working for weeks on end on a painting if it is not suitable for printing.'

In July 1990 Trevor was able to leave the Alderbourne Unit to marry and set up home with his wife Shirley who was his osteopath. Today Trevor and Shirley live busy lives at their home in Buckinghamshire. Apart from painting, Trevor has to visit the Association's headquarters in Vaduz in December and June each year in his role as member of the Association's Board. Although his accident put an end to his involvement in physical sports the old sporting thrill returned when he arranged to have his first flight in a glider – much to Shirley's misgiving.

'She's never been openly keen about flying in general but she thought it was a bit mad to go up in an aircraft with no engine,' Trevor explained. 'But I found it wonderful to fly over the beautiful terrain in silence apart from the slight hiss of the air over the wings.'

Talking about life with her husband Trevor, Shirley Wells once said, 'I am an osteopath and was once asked if I could treat someone in a wheelchair. I replied that it would be no problem and soon afterwards Trevor arrived. We rapidly became friends and very, very soon I no longer saw him in a wheelchair.

'A lot of people might think it mundane doing the little things that I have to do for him but it is the involvement that I like. We chat about things, discuss how a picture is going, what should be here and what should be there. This is much nicer than if you are married to a solicitor or someone like that where you cannot get involved with their work. When Trevor goes to exhibitions I obviously go with him and again I am involved. The public are quite surprised to find that we are just a normal couple – then they lose the wheelchair and see us as we really are.'

Cristobal Toledo   Portrait

TREVOR WELLS

Cristobal Toledo   Notre Dame, Paris

Cristobal Toledo   Gondolas, Venice

Cristobal Toledo   Red Blossoms in Vase

José Uribe
Still Life

José Uribe   Still Life with Fruit and Wine

José Uribe   Dome of the Cathedral in Compania

José Uribe   Still Life, Flowers in Vase

Overleaf
Trevor Wells
Forest Path

Trevor Wells   Winter's Day

Trevor Wells   Henley Bridge

Trevor Wells
By the River in Winter

Trevor Wells A Frosty Morning

ARTISTS WORLDWIDE

Trevor Wells
A Peaceful Village

Trevor Wells   Snowy Morning

Trevor Wells The Winter Trail